MW00622460

On Ordered Liberty

RELIGION, POLITICS, AND SOCIETY IN THE NEW MILLENNIUM

Series Editors: Michael Novak, American Enterprise Institute, and Brian C. Anderson, Manhattan Institute

For nearly five centuries, it was widely believed that moral questions could be resolved through reason. The Enlightenment once gave us answers to these perennial questions, but the answers no longer seem adequate. It has become apparent that reason alone is not enough to answer the questions that define and shape our existence. Many now believe that we have come to the edge of the Enlightenment and are stepping forth into a new era, one that may be the most religious we have experienced in 500 years. This series of books explores this new historical condition, publishing important works of scholarship in various disciplines that help us to understand the trends in thought and belief we have come from and to define the ones toward which we are heading.

Beyond Self-Interest: A Personalist Approach to Human Action, by Gregory R. Beabout, et al.

Human Nature and the Discipline of Economics: Personalist Anthropology and Economic Methodology, by Patricia Donohue-White, et al.

The Free Person and the Free Economy: A Personalist View of Market Economics, by Anthony J. Santelli Jr., et al.

Meaninglessness: The Solutions of Nietzsche, Freud, and Rorty, by M. A. Casey

Boston's Cardinal: Bernard Law, the Man and His Witness, edited by Romanus Cessario, O.P.

Don't Play Away Your Cards, Uncle Sam: The American Difference, by Olof Murelius, edited by Jana Novak

Society as a Department Store: Critical Reflections on the Liberal State, by Ryszard Legutko

In God We Trust? Faith-Based Organizations and the Quest to Solve America's Social Ills, by Lewis D. Solomon

Deconstructing Diversity: Justice, Multiculturalism, and Affirmative Action in Jesuit Higher Education, by Peter Minowitz

Relevant No More? The Catholic/Protestant Divide in American Electoral Politics, by Mark D. Brewer

On Ordered Liberty: A Treatise on the Free Society, by Samuel Gregg

On Ordered Liberty

A Treatise on the Free Society

Samuel Gregg

LEXINGTON BOOKS
Lanham • Boulder • New York • Oxford

LEXINGTON BOOKS

Published in the United States of America
by Lexington Books
An imprint of The Rowman & Littlefield Publishing Group, Inc.
4501 Forbes Boulevard, Suite 200, Lanham, Maryland 20706

PO Box 317
Oxford
OX2 9RU, UK

Copyright © 2003 by Lexington Books

All rights reserved. No part of this publication may be reproduced,
stored in a retrieval system, or transmitted in any form or by any
means, electronic, mechanical, photocopying, recording, or otherwise,
without the prior permission of the publisher.

British Library Cataloguing in Publication Information Available

Library of Congress Cataloging-in-Publication Data

Gregg, Samuel, 1969–
    On ordered liberty : a treatise on the free society / Samuel Gregg.
        p. cm. – (Religion, politics, and society in the new millennium)
    Includes index.
    ISBN 0-7391-0622-8 (cloth: alk. paper) – ISBN 0-7391-0668-6 (pbk.: alk. paper)
    1. Liberty. 2. Liberalism. 3. Liberty—Religious aspects. I. Title. II. Series.

JC585.G744 2003
320'.01'1—dc21   2003047471

Printed in the United States of America

♾™ The paper used in this publication meets the minimum requirements of American
National Standard for Information Sciences—Permanence of Paper for Printed Library
Materials, ANSI/NISO Z39.48–1992.

To the Glory of God

CONTENTS

Preface		xi
Acknowledgments		xv
1.	The Case for Liberty	1
2.	*Contra Ratio*: John Stuart Mill	13
3.	The Drama of Human Freedom	29
4.	Law and Liberty	51
5.	Whither the State?	69
6.	Little Platoons	89
7.	Reflections of a "Catholic Whig"	105
Index		121
About the Author		127

Men qualify for civil liberty in exact proportion to their disposition to put moral chains upon their own appetites; in proportion as their love of justice is above their rapacity; in proportion as their soundness and sobriety of understanding is above their vanity and presumption; in proportion as they are more disposed to listen to the counsels of the wise and good, in preference to the flattery of knaves. Society cannot exist unless a controlling power upon will and appetite be placed somewhere, and the less of it there is within, the more there must be without. It is ordained in the eternal constitution of things that men of intemperate minds cannot be free. Their passions forge their fetters.

—Edmund Burke

Order and order alone definitively makes liberty: Disorder makes servitude.

—Charles Péguy

PREFACE

The only liberty I mean is a liberty connected with order, that not only exists along with order and virtue, but which cannot exist at all without them.

—Edmund Burke[1]

Many would agree that the two most powerful visions of the future articulated during the nineteenth century were those of Karl Marx and Alexis de Tocqueville. If true, then the latter seems to have triumphed. Communism's collapse in East-Central Europe and the former Soviet Union would have delighted this French aristocrat who, in his later years, identified the emerging Socialist movements as a new threat to liberty.

Tocqueville himself, however, grew distinctly pessimistic in later life about the future of freedom. Upon returning from America in 1832, the author of the seminal texts *Democracy in America* and *L'Ancien Régime et la Révolution* entered the political world of Orleanist France. To his chagrin, de Tocqueville found the experience frustrating. Too few politicians grasped the accuracy of his intuition that the French Revolution's destruction of aristocratic power, its assault on the Catholic Church, and its centralization of State authority had effectively destroyed the main institutions protecting local autonomy. French society was therefore in a poor condition to nurture and maintain free institutions. This became evident following the collapse of the regime of Louis Philippe, better known as the "Citizen-King," in 1848. The succeeding Second French Republic successfully resisted the attempts of Jacobin and Socialist agitators to destroy the new democracy, only to be extinguished by the coup d'état launched by the President of the Republic, Napoleon's nephew, Louis-Napoleon Bonaparte, in 1851.

The world of de Tocqueville's France, a society characterized by chronic political instability, seems very distant as we look back from the cusp of the twenty-first century. By comparison, democratic societies of the West seem remarkably steady. Yet perhaps de Tocqueville's greatest insight was that the more insidious threats to freedom in the democratic future would not be from external enemies or those harboring authoritarian inclinations. A core message of his *Democracy in America* is that free societies will endure internal decline if the vital *mores* of freedom were eroded. "It cannot," de Tocqueville insisted, "be repeated too often: Nothing is more fertile than the art of being free, but nothing is harder than freedom's apprenticeship."[2]

Tocqueville's warning may have sounded odd to the people of his time. Yet, as the experience of Weimar Germany illustrates, the most finely crafted constitutional democracy will not last if its people are insufficiently schooled in the responsibilities of freedom. The purpose of this book is to make a modest contribution to this end by introducing the reader to some of the underlying philosophical debates about the character of freedom, and to articulate an idea of liberty and the free society that seeks to meet the demands of practical reason. And, by "practical reason," I do not mean what is efficient or workable. Rather, practical reason involves thinking about what we ought to do when making choices and acting in general.[3]

Any treatise on the free society involves attempting to clarify "what we mean" when we speak of liberty. To crystallize the contemporary intellectual divisions about the nature of freedom, this book begins by delineating the abyss of interpretation of the word *liberty* that separates two self-described English liberals of the nineteenth century, Lord Acton and John Stuart Mill.

As readers proceed through successive chapters, they will quickly discern that the author is firmly in the "Actonian" camp. This reflects the reasoned conviction that each person who possesses unimpaired reason *is* capable of knowing truth, and that without truth, genuine free choice is an impossibility. Here it is worth noting that nothing in this book is defended by an appeal to the authority of any institution or person. Appeals to such authority do have their place. They are not, however, appropriate in philosophical argument about the nature of liberty.

Those trained in political and moral theory will recognize that this book owes a significant intellectual debt to two primary sources. The first source is the reflections of de Tocqueville. The questions he asked about the world bequeathed by the events of 1789 remain perennially relevant to any reflection about liberty.

The second source is the fundamental moral theory associated with the work of the theologian Germain Grisez and the jurists, John Finnis and Robert P. George. This book does not add any new insights to their ideas (sometimes referred to as the "new natural law" school). It attempts, however, to introduce readers to the basic premises of their theory, precisely because of its ability to speak about human liberty in ways that accord with man's moral reality. The idea of freedom articulated by Grisez, Finnis, and George as well as by this book, is best described as "self-mastery," "integral fulfillment," or, more simply, "integral liberty."

These primary reference points should not, however, obscure the fact that this book engages the work of several thinkers who identify themselves as "liberal." Readers will quickly recognize that I regard many liberal contributions to ideas about liberty as incoherent and reliant upon a series of rationalizations. Nonetheless, important insights contained in these writings can be integrated into the project of ordered liberty.

Beyond these considerations of philosophical presentation and disputation, this book also endeavors to remind us why liberty is important. In doing so, it suggests that the primary defense of the free society is not to be found in terms of its greater material prosperity. Instead, the fundamental justifications for the free society—including its economic dimension—lie in the moral realm. Only when this is understood will we be better placed to defend the free society against more subtle threats.

It is unlikely, for example, that Western societies will be faced, at least in the short term, with a crisis of the type that paralyzed Europe in the 1930s. The naked will to power of a Stalin or Hitler does not loom as an immediate danger. The contemporary menaces to liberty are more elusive. At their heart is an often-unconscious reliance upon the methods and principles of utilitarian philosophy by not only most Western thinkers but by large numbers of the general population.

Addressing these problems is a more complex exercise than confronting the Marxist-Leninist regimes of yesteryear. The Cold War provided many who professed to love liberty with a common foe, and reasons to temporarily suspend some of their disagreements about the character of freedom.

Yet, in another sense, nothing has changed. Some of the basic questions shaping our understanding of liberty and its implications for the social order remain constant. The hubristic delusion that man can recreate the world from a *tabula rasa* has not disappeared. Even more fundamentally, man continues to confront the fact that, as the twentieth-century German economist Wilhelm Röpke once wrote, "We have, for the past century, made the desperate attempt to get along without God, and in the place of God we have set up the cult of man, his profane or even ungodly science and art, his technical achievements, and his State."[4]

Religious belief is not a precondition for appreciating the ideas about liberty articulated in the first six chapters of this book. On the one hand, nonbelieving readers may wish to limit themselves to these sections without concerning themselves with the concluding chapter. On the other hand, the final chapter may provide them with insights into the issues with which believers who value freedom must grapple in the pluralist conditions of modern secular liberal democracies.

Of course, ours is not the first time during which many in the West have sought to live as if God does not exist. We need only recall the atheism of many of the French *philosophes* who dominated eighteenth-century European intellectual life. Nonetheless, for all the prevailing skepticism, most people of the time—educated and humble—continued to believe in a divine order. They also believed that their actions in the here-and-now affected their destiny beyond this world.

The contrast today could not be more stark. Few people would describe themselves as atheistic materialists. Yet, many who call themselves Jews or Christians appear to presume upon divine benevolence, believe that God can be effortlessly appeased or bought off, and have no time for any warnings about the alienation from God that is inherent in immorality and potentially final. This phenomenon is what Plato referred to over two thousand years ago as one of the three varieties of practical atheism: to live and act as if God does not exist (*si Deus non daretur*).[5] It also threatens one of the most consistent messages articulated by the synthesis of Athens, Jerusalem, and Rome that lies at the very heart of Western civilization: that moral truth and freedom are indivisible.

The sundering of this link represents the most significant threat to liberty in our time.

Notes

1. Edmund Burke, "Speech at Mr. Burke's Arrival in Bristol (1774)," in *The Portable Edmund Burke*, ed. I. Kramnick (London: Penguin Books, 1999), 155.

2. Alexis de Tocqueville, *Democracy in America*, ed. J. P. Mayer, trans. G. Lawrence (New York: Perennial Classics, 2000), 40.

3. See John Finnis, *Natural Law and Natural Rights* (Oxford: Clarendon Press, 1980), 12. See also Aristotle, *Nicomachean Ethics*, trans. J. A. K. Thomson (London: Penguin Classics, 1976), VI, 2: 139a26–31.

4. Wilhelm Röpke, *A Humane Economy: The Social Framework of the Free Market* (Wilmington, Del.: ISI Books, 1998), 8.

5. See Plato, *The Laws* (Harmondsworth: Penguin Classics, 1991), X, 885b, 888c, 901d, 902e–903a, 908b–d, 909a–b.

ACKNOWLEDGMENTS

The completion of this book has fulfilled a desire to explore a perennial question in a way that hopefully allows others to reflect upon a philosophical issue that lies at the root of so many contemporary political debates. While the analysis and narrative of *On Ordered Liberty* are my responsibility, the contribution and counsel of various individuals is gratefully acknowledged.

The bulk of this text was written in the United States. This happy event is due to the kind invitation of the Acton Institute to join its staff in 2001. Its conviction that the world needs societies that are both free and virtuous has inspired many people to synthesize more adequately their concern for liberty with the demands of truth.

Thanks are also extended to Michael Novak, gentleman, scholar, and quintessential Catholic Whig, for his advice over several years. My editor at Lexington Books, Serena Krombach, is thanked for her patience and help.

Also to be acknowledged are those with whom, over the past few years, I have discussed many of the issues examined in *On Ordered Liberty*. For their contributions, both witting and unwitting, I thank Thomas Behr, Bill Campbell, Michael Casey, Ricardo Crespo, Phillip De Vous, John Eddy, John Finnis, Stephen Grabill, Ian Harper, Robert G. Kennedy, Jan Klos, Santiago Legarre, Greg Lindsay, Tony Macken, Kris Alan Mauren, John McCarthy, Marshal and Teresa McMahon, Doug Ollivant, Tony Percy, Jennifer Roback Morse, Robert A. Sirico, Kevin Schmiesing, Manfred Spieker, Max Torres, George Weigel, Rachel Wondergem, Jerry Zandstra, Christof Zellenberg, and Gloria Zúñiga.

Though my mother, Jeannette Gregg, and sisters, Sarah and Susannah Gregg, live at such great distance from me, their support for my work is never in doubt.

Lastly, I thank Ingrid Merikoski for her support, her comments, and her care. My debt to her is inestimable. *Claritatis pulchritudinem.*

Finally, readers of this book should observe the following caveat: Whatever truth it contains is His. The errors are mine.

1

The Case for Liberty

If old truths are to retain their hold on men's minds, they must be restated in the language and concepts of successive generations. What at one time are their most effective expressions gradually become so worn with use that they cease to carry a definite meaning. The underlying ideas may be as valid as ever, but the words, even when they refer to problems that are still with us, no longer convey the same conviction; the arguments do not move in a context familiar to us; and they rarely give direct answers to the questions we are asking.

—Friedrich von Hayek[1]

The nineteenth century may be described as the century of "liberalism." By this, we do not mean that a cohesive movement called "liberalism" emerged across the world. For the word *liberalism* is a wonderfully pliant term. It is used to label a range of philosophical and religious positions, many of which have little in common. Both the political theorist John Rawls and the economist Friedrich von Hayek, for example, are commonly described as "liberals." Yet, it is difficult to imagine two individuals whose views on many matters are more opposed to each other. This only underlines the fact that it makes little sense to ask whether a set of proposed practices and principles are "liberal" or, for that matter, "conservative." Reasoned inquiry should ask whether an idea is reasonable and therefore true, or unreasonable and thus untrue.

1

The nineteenth century may nonetheless be characterized as an age of liberalism insofar as some of the most significant writing commonly denoted as liberal was penned in this period. In such works, we find many powerful contributions to the eventual legal recognition of important human freedoms. Among the most prominent of these nineteenth-century "liberals" were John Emirich Dalberg-Acton and John Stuart Mill.

Two Liberals

Acton and Mill brought quite different inheritances to their vision of the world, much of which influenced their somewhat dissimilar views of liberty. A historian and political thinker, Acton was a prominent figure in the intellectual and political life of Victorian England. A devout Catholic, this scion of prominent English gentry as well as one of the Holy Roman Empire's most aristocratic families was primarily educated at the University of Munich (1850–1857) under the tutorship of the historian Ignaz von Döllinger. Much contemporary fascination with Acton derives from the manner in which he integrated his Catholicism with a commitment to political liberalism. In the service of these ideas, Acton wrote numerous articles on topics ranging from continental nationalism to the American Civil War. To this activity may be added Acton's brief period in the House of Commons (1859–1865), before his elevation to the House of Lords by the Liberal Prime Minister of Britain, William Gladstone.

Much of Acton's energies in the late 1860s were consumed by the debates within the Roman Catholic Church concerning the dogma of Papal Infallibility. Defeated on this issue at the First Vatican Council, Acton focused upon private historical studies, with his 1877 lectures on "The History of Freedom in Antiquity" and "The History of Freedom in Christianity" foreshadowing his unrealized ambition of writing a tomelike *History of Liberty*. On the basis of such contributions as well as his reputation for learnedness, Acton was appointed Regius Professor of History at Cambridge in 1895, holding the position until his death in 1902.

Acton's aristocratic background permitted him to move easily in that cosmopolitan world of the nobility that transcended European nation-state boundaries. He thus had an appreciation for traditions of liberty that originated outside the English experience. Hence, unlike most of his fellow Englishmen, Acton acknowledged Saint Thomas Aquinas's significance for the development of thinking about political freedom. Nor did Acton make the common mistake of grounding the development of free institutions more or less solely in the post-Reformation world. He also grasped the central role played by Judaism and early Christianity in deabsolutizing the State by refusing to accord divine status to the

Caesars, the spirit of which was captured in the cry of an early Christian martyr: *Deus major est, non imperatores* [God is the greater One, not the emperors]!

Though a contemporary of Acton, John Stuart Mill's education was very different, not least because of Mill's more limited exposure to non–Anglo-Saxon philosophers. Moreover, unlike Acton, Mill was profoundly influenced by the philosophy of Jeremy Bentham and other utilitarian thinkers. This remained, for the rest of his life, a primary reference point.

Mill's study abroad amounted to one year in the south of France in Montpellier, where he stayed with Sir Samuel Bentham (brother of Jeremy). Upon his return to England in 1821, Mill read the works of the French philosopher Abbé Etienne de Condillac while studying law under the father of modern legal positivism, John Austin. Through contact with men like Austin, Mill was initiated into English utilitarian circles, so much so that he spent most of 1825 editing Bentham's five volume *Rationale of Evidence*.

Prolonged overwork, culminating in the editing of Bentham's manuscripts, resulted in Mill's experiencing a nervous breakdown that same year. In this period of dejection, Benthamite utilitarianism lost some of its charm for Mill. He concluded that the emphasis placed by Bentham and the French *philosophes* on utility—"the principle which approves or disapproves of every action whatsoever, according to the tendency it appears to have to augment or diminish the happiness of the party whose interest is in question"[2]—should be supplemented by an awareness of other aspects of human life. This may account for Mill's later writings on religion. Approaching the subject as a sociological phenomenon, Mill noted that he "was bought up from the first without any religious belief, in the ordinary acceptation of the term."[3] Though Mill's evaluation of the arguments for God's existence amounted "only to one of the lower degrees of probability,"[4] he did not think that the alternative was to try to realize heaven-on-earth or to attribute man with the characteristics of a god. Mill did, nonetheless, confess his frustration that "ordinary human nature is so poor a thing."[5]

Between 1829 and 1865, Mill established himself as a noted philosopher in his own right by writing works such as *Utilitarianism* (1863), *Principles of Political Economy* (1848), and, perhaps most famously, *On Liberty* (1859). He entered the House of Commons the same year that Acton departed for the Lords. Like Acton, Mill supported the 1867 Reform Act, which gave the vote to every male adult householder living in a borough constituency, and Home Rule for Ireland as a way of resolving that unhappy island's problems while keeping it within the British Empire.

Both Mill and Acton were thus intimately involved in the political debates of their time, but the primary intellectual interest dominating their lives was not any, one, particular policy question. Rather, their consuming passion was *liberty:* its origins, nature, and purposes.

Liberty or Liberty?

As one who devoted his life to history, Acton recognized that the idea of freedom was incomprehensible without recognizing the respective contributions of Judaism, Christianity, and the world of Greece and Rome to fostering its development. Yet while conscious of the historical-cultural sources of freedom, Acton was also attentive to the philosophical dimension. When speaking of liberty in this sense, he offered several definitions. In his "History of Freedom in Antiquity," Acton wrote:

> By "liberty" I mean the assurance that every man shall be protected in doing what he believes is his duty against the influence of authority and majorities, custom and opinion. The State is competent to assign duties and draw the line between good and evil only in its immediate sphere. Beyond the limits of things necessary for its well-being, it can only give indirect help to fight the battle of life by promoting the influences which prevail against temptation—religion, education.[6]

Though Acton never elaborated upon his preferred constitutional framework, he evidently associated liberty with some form of commitment to limited government. On many occasions, Acton expounded the benefits of constitutional orders that divided political power. Significantly, he stressed Aquinas's contribution to the provision of substantive intellectual underpinning to such an order.[7] "[T]he politics of the Neapolitan friar," Acton commented, "are centuries in advance of the English statesman's."[8] A more recent affirmation of this observation may be found in the works of the jurist John Finnis:

> We could accept that the first liberal ("the first Whig") was Thomas Aquinas ... because, although he rightly defended institutions and practices important in public life on the basis that they are required or authorized by certain moral and metaphysical *truths*, he at the same time insisted that the proper function of the State's laws and rulers does not include making people morally all-round good.... The role of State government and law, according to Aquinas, is to uphold peace and justice: The requirements imposed, supervised, and enforced by state government and law concern only those sorts of choice and action which are external and affect other people.[9]

Neither Acton nor Finnis believe that the State has no role to play in shaping what some have called the *moral ecology* of society. Where the limits of legitimate coercion lie in this regard is a subject for debate. Yet, while neither Finnis nor Acton could even remotely be regarded as a moral relativist, both recognize that the element of free choice is critical if a human act is to be authentically free.

Acton's antirelativism is most apparent in his linkage of liberty with duty. This is most evident in his famous definition of liberty as "not the power of doing what we like, but the right of being able to do what we ought."[10]

There was nothing especially radical about this definition in which the word *ought* features so prominently. In his Letter to the Romans, Saint Paul speaks of people becoming slaves to sin (Rom. 7:7–13) when they act in ways which they *know* they ought not to act. Aristotle also understood freedom as being directed toward human flourishing in the sense of acquiring virtue. Both, in short, viewed freedom as inseparable from knowledge of the proper ends of human action (the good). They also believed that people could discern, if dimly, such ends through their reason, and then freely choose to act in ways that attain these ends without engaging in evil.

The understanding of the relationship between reason and free will that underlies Acton's concept of liberty conflicts sharply with that of the eighteenth-century Scottish Enlightenment thinker, David Hume. The latter maintained that "Reason is and ought to be the slave of the passions and may never pretend to any other office than to serve and obey them."[11] In Hume's view, reason's role is not to identify what is rational—that is, what people should want or ought to do—but merely to devise means of obtaining goals that people simply desire. In making this statement, Hume may have been attempting to deflate the hubristic tendencies encouraged by the rationalism articulated by French Enlightenment *philosophes*, but in doing so, he effectively reduced reason to the level of an instrument, a reduction that assumes that reason cannot vindicate any fundamental principles. Nowhere, however, does Hume provide any proofs to demonstrate the validity of this assumption.

This Humean understanding of reason, free will, and desire is implicit to Mill's writings about the nature of freedom. "Liberty consists," Mill wrote, "in doing what one desires."[12] This sentiment is further echoed in Mill's comment that "In the part, which merely concerns himself, his independence is, of right, absolute. Over himself, over his own body and mind, the individual is sovereign."[13]

Such language might be easily employed by an anarchist or a libertine, though Mill was neither. The mere fact that a person desires something provides for Mill at least prima facie justification for an act. Little consideration is given to whether such a desire is reasonable or otherwise. "Ought," for Mill, is a more limited concept, its primary expression being the principle that we ought not to interfere in others' liberty, unless their actions cause harm to others.

To be fair to Mill, we should note that by "liberty" he did not mean merely freedom from external control. Mill believed, for example, that liberty involved the freedom to develop oneself as a human being in the "full sense," a freedom demanded by what Mill called the "common good." These are important qualifications. Nevertheless, what constituted a human being "in the full sense" or what is the content of the "common good" were questions that Mill did not answer. In part, Mill did not do so because, as we will see, the principle of utility—the lodestone of utilitarian logic—is unable to answer questions such as "What is a human being" or "What is authentic human fulfillment?"

As if recognizing these problems in his thought, Mill's Humean-utilitarian concept of man was considerably nuanced by his simultaneous if somewhat uncertain embrace of an idea of the individual seeking to develop all his powers and skills. To this end, Mill was prepared to sanction a range of State-sponsored legislation to remove obstacles to this self-development. He insisted, however, on justifying this according to the "greatest happiness of the greatest number" principle. On this premise, Mill claimed, "Is it not almost a self-evident axiom that the State should require and compel the education, up to a certain standard, of every human being who is born its citizen?"[14]

Unfortunately for Mill, the principle on which he bases this claim requires some form of measurement of the total sum of human happiness. The utility principle dictates that this is to be found in the maximization of pleasure and the minimizing of pain. As will become apparent, measuring such things is impossible.

An Exploration of Freedom

The chasm that separates Acton and Mill's respective understandings of freedom is that which separates freedom as a willed and reasoned liberty (*voluntas*) from liberty of appetite (*libido*). Their divergent positions proceed from a range of differing conclusions about the nature of man, most particularly the character of his reason. They also reflect differing views on what the Roman scholar Cicero understood as the ultimate debate over the ends of human life. "There remains," Cicero wrote, "one match to be fought off—pleasure versus moral worth."[15] Which way of life accords with the reality of man?

The purpose of this book is not to provide an all-encompassing resolution to such questions. In part, it is to illustrate that much of the modern case for freedom is encumbered by a continuing reliance, implicit or otherwise, upon utilitarian premises and methodology. In chapter 2, the comparison of Hayek and Rawls illustrates how two twentieth-century liberals were unable, despite their avowed desire to do so, to dispense with such assumptions and methods.

A consequent objective of this book is to present a case for liberty—a liberty ordered by reason rather than by preference—that provides answers to questions concerning why man should be free, answers that transcend appeals to a calculus of pleasure and pain. These explanations are then applied to the subjects of law, the State, and civil society. Here, we consider some of the genuine problems surrounding the establishment of a commitment to liberty within the social order, and we consider how such issues might be resolved.

Many of the questions asked in this book are derived from reflection upon de Tocqueville's insights into the dilemmas confronting man in the modern age. Tocqueville is, of course, a figure from the world of nineteenth-century liberalism. But as his biographer, André Jardin, observes, much of the continuing fascination with de Tocqueville is that he "was a liberal not like the others."[16] In the midst of great liberal optimism and faith in progress, de Tocqueville continued to ask how freedom might be preserved in the face of new dangers only then just becoming perceivable to man.

More than one twentieth-century scholar identifying himself as "liberal" has wrestled with the quandaries predicted by de Tocqueville. Liberal scholars such as Rawls, Hayek, the jurist Joseph Raz, and the political theorist William Galston have all drawn our attention to developments that anyone thinking about the nature of a free society must take into account. One example might be the continuing expansion of options for choice and the subsequent emergence of very pluralist societies. How, then, do we resolve the inevitable conflicts between many people's choices in a manner consistent with a commitment to liberty and justice? Many liberals have embraced the solution of another nineteenth-century French liberal, the philosopher and politician Benjamin Constant, who stressed that basic principles acceptable to all parties must replace the rule of belligerent ideologies.[17] Much depends, of course, on what is meant by "basic principles" and whether or not they are understood to be derived from reason seeking truth or from a simple consensus of opinion.

It is difficult to imagine a time when clear thinking about such matters was more urgently required. Within much of the Academy, the collapse of Marxist-Leninist regimes throughout the world has not spurred a return to the classical foundations of Western thought. Instead, throughout much of the West, we have witnessed the ongoing flourishing of two views. The first, championed by figures such as the French thinker Michel Foucault, is the neo-Marxist view that everything can be understood in terms of the exercise of power by one or more groups over others. The second is the conclusion that knowledge of truth is essentially a futile exercise. Concerning the latter, the philosopher John Searle claims that in the universities there are challenges "not just to the content of the curriculum but to the very concepts of rationality, truth, objectivity, and reality that have been taken for granted in higher education, as they have been taken for granted in our civilization at large." These qualities, Searle states, are rejected "*even as ideals.*"[18] In 1998, we witnessed the remarkable spectacle of the head of the Catholic Church issuing an encyclical letter defending the Catholic conviction that human reason can seek and find truth.[19] Given his lampooning of the Catholic Church as a bastion of ignorance and superstition, one suspects that the eighteenth-century *philosophe*, François Marie Arouet (better known to history as Voltaire), would turn in his grave if he knew that the foremost defender of reason and truth at the end of the twentieth century was the Bishop of Rome.

In 1960, Hayek opined that a revival of freedom meant that "[s]o far as the West is concerned, we must hope here there still exists wide consent on certain fundamental values."[20] In present circumstances, this hope might seem excessively optimistic. In his important 1981 book, *After Virtue*, the philosopher Alasdair MacIntyre despaired that Western societies had largely lost the capacity to reflect reasonably upon moral and political issues.[21] Words like "morality," "virtue," "reason," and "will," he argued, are widely used without any real appreciation of the classical context of such terms and the manner in which they relate to each other. Their meaning has been obscured by the establishment of what MacIntyre describes as "emotivism" as an orthodoxy among Western philosophers and public discourse as a whole. By "emotivism," MacIntyre has in mind the idea that there is no such thing as "good" and that when people use such phrases, "they are doing no more and no other than expressing their feelings and attitudes, disguising the expression of preference and whim by an interpretation of their own utterance and behavior, which confers upon it an objectivity that it does not in fact possess."[22] Hence, we should hardly be surprised to hear philosophers such as John Mackie announcing that "there are no objective values."[23]

The real danger of these developments is that if we concede that people may define themselves and act simply as they prefer, it becomes harder to resist the notion that some people should be able to treat others as they prefer. Herein lies the terrible ambiguity of modern freedom. It can result in man's making himself a law unto himself.

Restating a Tradition

It would indeed be easy to despair in such circumstances or to dwell upon the obstacles that hinder the flourishing of liberty properly understood. The tradition of liberty is not, however, the exclusive creation of any one person, country, or period. The very act of restating the case for an ordered liberty can have unforeseen positive consequences. When the eighteenth-century Whig parliamentarian Edmund Burke took the step of arguing that the French Revolution would eventually diminish the necessary conditions for human liberty, he was mocked by many. In his *Rights of Man*, the American revolutionary Thomas Paine castigated Burke for his "pathless wilderness of rhapsodies . . . a sort of descant upon Governments, in which he asserts whatever he pleases."[24] The French, Paine claimed, were in the process of giving themselves a rational, equitable established Constitution, whereas that of Britain, so extolled by Burke, was nothing but a haphazard anthology of unjust customs based on no better claim than conquest by a Norman adventurer.[25]

Not only was Burke vindicated (as he predicted, the Revolution *did* result in war, institutionalized State terrorism, and eventually military dictatorship), but his work provided the necessary stimulus for others to engage in an intellectual critique of a phenomenon that shook all of Europe. Even those who disagreed with aspects of Burke's analysis, such as his Prussian translator Friedrich Gentz, were profoundly influenced by the rigor of Burke's critique and forced to reconsider their initial enthusiasm for the Revolution. In a similar fashion, Hayek's 1944 publication, *The Road to Serfdom* galvanized those concerned about the spread of the tendency to regard State economic intervention as the universal cure-all for social problems as World War II drew to a close.[26]

This book makes no claim to being the catalyst of a far-reaching renewal of thought about freedom and the free society. It does, however, seek to introduce the core ideas of a certain concept of liberty—what we will call *integral liberty*—to audiences accustomed to thinking primarily about freedom in terms of the "positive liberty" and "negative liberty" proposed by the liberal thinker Sir Isaiah Berlin. In doing so, it illustrates that many arguments about the nature of freedom derive from serious disagreement about the correct answer to the question, *Quid sit Homo?* What, indeed, is man?

The significance of an accurate answer to this question goes beyond that of resolving philosophical disputes. It has profound political, social, and economic implications. This point was made forcibly by John Paul II in his 1991 encyclical letter *Centesimus Annus*. Reflecting upon the collapse of Communism, he wrote:

> The fundamental error of socialism is *anthropological* in nature. Socialism considers the individual person simply as an element, a molecule within the social organism, so that the good of the individual is completely subordinated to the functioning of the socio-economic mechanism. Socialism likewise maintains that the good of the individual can be realized without reference to *his free choice, to the unique and exclusive responsibility which he exercises in the face of good or evil.* Man is thus reduced to a series of social relationships, and the concept of the person as *the autonomous subject of moral decision* disappears, the very subject whose decisions build the social order.[27]

Socialism failed because it sought to ignore certain *truths* about the person. The extract above refers to the folly of building a socio-economic system, which denies that man possesses the unique faculty of free choice. Attempts to build a social order based on the claim that free choice must be suppressed in the name of economic equality will therefore eventually turn to dust, though not before much unnecessary suffering and hardship for millions.

If human freedom is to be rational freedom, it must be grounded in what man is, rather than on a fantasy or fiction. Even more particularly, it must be based upon a correct understanding of the relationship between the human reason, free will, and desires that are operative within each of us as embodied human persons. These questions intrude inevitably upon the metaphysical, a realm of knowledge largely neglected by significant numbers of Western thinkers for the past four centuries.

Prominent among those who rejected metaphysics was John Stuart Mill. Though aspects of Mill's thought may be admired, it has also burdened the movement for freedom with the historical incubus of an incoherent philosophical system that has the potential to decisively weaken resistance to the growth of arbitrary power. We must therefore persuade those who love the free society that nothing less than a complete repudiation of utilitarianism is required if a regime of ordered liberty is to endure.

Notes

1. Friedrich Hayek, *The Constitution of Liberty* (London: Routledge & Kegan Paul, 1960), 1.

2. Jeremy Bentham, *An Introduction to the Principles of Morals and Legislation*, ed. L. K. Lafleur (Oxford: Basil Blackwell, 1948), c. 1, sec. 2.

3. John Stuart Mill, *Autobiography*, ed. H. J. Laski (New York: Oxford University Press, 1952), 38.

4. John Stuart Mill, *Three Essays on Religion* (Bristol: Thoemmes Press, 1993), 102.

5. John Stuart Mill, "The Claims of Labor," *Dissertations and Discussions*, vol. 2 (New York: E. P. Dutton & Co., 1905), 288.

6. John Dalberg-Acton, "The History of Freedom in Antiquity," in *Selected Writings of Lord Acton*, vol. 1, *Essays in the History of Liberty*, ed. J. R. Fears (Indianapolis: Liberty Classics, 1986), 7.

7. See, for example, John Dalberg-Acton, "The History of Freedom in Christianity," in *Essays in the History of Liberty*, 34.

8. Acton, "History of Freedom in Christianity," 34.

9. John Finnis, "The Catholic Church and Public Policy Debates in Western Liberal Societies," in *Issues for a Catholic Bioethic*, ed. L. Gormally (London: Linacre Center, 1997), 261. See also Saint Thomas Aquinas, *Summa Theologiae* (London: Blackfriars, 1975), II-II, q. 104, a. 5.

10. John Dalberg-Acton, *Selected Writings of Lord Acton*, vol. 3, *Essays in Religion, Politics, and Morality*, ed. J. R. Fears (Indianapolis: Liberty Classics, 1988), 613.

11. David Hume, *A Treatise of Human Nature: Being an Attempt to Introduce the Experimental Method of Reasoning into Moral Subjects*, ed. L. Selby-Bigge (Oxford: Oxford University Press, 1738–40/1951), bk. 2, pt. 3, sec. 3.

12. John Stuart Mill, *On Liberty, Considerations on Representative Government*, ed. R. B. McCallum (Oxford: Oxford University Press, 1946), 118.

13. Mill, *On Liberty*, 9.

14. Ibid., 94.

15. Cicero, *Academica*, trans. H. Rackham (London: Loeb Classical Library, 1933), 2.46.140.

16. André Jardin, *Tocqueville: A Biography* (New York: Farrar Straus Giroux, 1988), 535.

17. See Benjamin Constant, *De la force du gouvernement actuel de la France et de la nécessité de s'y rallier*, ed. P. Raynaud (Paris: Flammarion, 1988), 131.

18. John R. Searle, "Rationality and Realism: What Is at Stake?" *Daedalus* (Fall 1993): 55.

19. See John Paul II, Encyclical Letter *Fides et Ratio* (London: Catholic Truth Society, 1998).

20. Hayek, *Constitution*, 3.

21. See Alasdair MacIntyre, *After Virtue: A Study in Moral Theory* (Notre Dame: University of Notre Dame Press, 1981), 22–59.

22. MacIntyre, *After Virtue*, 16–17.

23. John Mackie, *Ethics: Inventing Right and Wrong* (New York: Penguin Books, 1977), 15.

24. See Thomas Paine, *Rights of Man, Common Sense, and Other Political Writings*, ed. Mark Philip (Oxford: Oxford University Press, 1998), 25.

25. Paine, *Rights of Man*, 27.

26. See Richard Cockett, *Thinking the Unthinkable: Think-Tanks and the Economic Counter-Revolution, 1931–1983* (London: HarperCollins, 1995); and R. M. Hartwell, *A History of the Mont Pèlerin Society* (Indianapolis: Liberty Fund, 1995).

27. John Paul II, Encyclical Letter *Centesimus Annus* (London: Catholic Truth Society, 1991), par. 13 (emphasis added).

2

Contra Ratio: John Stuart Mill

> *Habits of thought useful in action are not always helpful to thought.*
>
> —Alexis de Tocqueville[1]

The intellectual world in which John Stuart Mill lived was one marked by upheaval, turbulence, and increasing fracture. This was perhaps most marked in nineteenth-century English theological and ecclesiastical circles. Within the Church of England, the theological cleavages between Tractarians such as E. B. Pusey, liberals of the likes of Renn Dickson Hampden, and Evangelicals became more distinct. The Elizabethan settlement of the sixteenth century, which had created a national Church combining Catholic ritual and hierarchy with Protestant doctrines and anti-Romanism, finally broke down. This was evident from the significant number of prominent conversions by intellectuals and aristocrats to Catholicism and from the large masses of people entering the ever-proliferating Dissenting chapels of Methodism.

The intensity of the subsequent debates cannot be underestimated. One need only read an 1829 letter in which the-then Oxford Tractarian and later Catholic cardinal, John Henry Newman, identifies those within the English intellectual tradition whom he believed to be in error. These included utilitarians, republicans, deists, Baptists, and "indifferentists." All were infected by what Newman called "a spirit that tends to overthrow doctrine."[2] Even as an old man, tempered by his involvement in the fierce debates surrounding papal infallibility, Newman

13

did not hesitate to denounce liberalism in religion. In his 1879 *biglietto* speech delivered on the occasion of being created a cardinal, Newman gently reminded his listeners that "for thirty, forty, fifty years I have resisted to the best of my powers the spirit of liberalism in religion [which] is an error overspreading, as a snare, the whole earth."[3] While Newman was prepared to state that "there is much in the liberalistic theory which is good and true," he maintained that it was precisely because of these positive aspects that "[t]here never was a device of the Enemy, so cleverly framed, and with such promise of success as liberalism in religion."[4] Liberalism's encouragement of reliance on private judgment by believer and nonbeliever alike is satirized by Newman in his portrait of the British and Foreign Truth Society in his 1847 novel, *Loss and Gain*. This gathering of erudites holds fast to two unquestionable dogmas: It is unsure whether truth exists; and it is sure that truth cannot be known.[5]

Outside the rarified atmosphere of high theology, a similar ferment of ideas was under way in English political and economic life. The 1832 Reform Act undermined the hold of the aristocracy and gentry on political power by widening the franchise and abolishing various corrupt practices. The repeal of the protectionist Corn Laws in 1846, the subsequent expansion of free trade, and accelerating industrialization rapidly changed patterns of life that had remained relatively constant since the Middle Ages.

In an atmosphere of such flux, the potential for a philosopher to influence the intellectual culture decisively was great. It is no coincidence that Marxism established a firm grip on the minds of many continental Europeans in the wake of the turmoil unleashed by industrialization as well as by the political tumult proceeding from the French Revolution.

In England, however, it was not Marxism that enjoyed intellectual success. Mill's utilitarianism proved far more influential. In retrospect, this is not difficult to understand. Utilitarianism's claim to encapsulate a universal but secular and scientific ethical system of humanitarian social reform was bound to be of great appeal in an age of profound scientific discovery, of unprecedented economic development, and of growing doubts about the claims of Christianity in the wake of Darwinism.

Since Mill's time, much of the intellectual climate of the Anglo-Saxon world has been profoundly shaped by this utilitarian mould. Several early Socialists relied upon utilitarian premises, and Mill himself was slowly moved in this political direction by the own logic of his thought. Many modern liberals continue to base their ideas on essentially utilitarian premises, as illustrated in the common tendency to regard a person's preferences as, prima facie, a legitimate basis for action. Many would agree with the claim of the legal and political philosopher, Robert P. George, that by the mid-1960s, "the spirit of Mill's philosophy had, perhaps, acquired the status of orthodoxy among an academic elite."[6]

Hume, Bentham, and the Calculus of Pleasure

As noted, much of Mill's utilitarian philosophy was derived from reflection upon Jeremy Bentham's writings. Bentham should not, however, be viewed in isolation. He drew principal inspiration from two sources. One was the Continental Enlightenment dream that emerged in the seventeenth and eighteenth centuries of creating a world in which suffering is abolished through the consistent application of scientific reason to every dimension of life.[7] A second influence was the thought of David Hume. In his *Fragment on Government*,[8] Bentham specifically acknowledged how illuminating he found Hume's claim that, in the final analysis, every virtue is derived from *utility*. In another place, Hume went so far as to state that "public utility is the sole origin of justice."[9]

Bentham's utilitarianism also appears to have been shaped by Hume's idea of how human beings determine what is good and evil. "The hypothesis which we embrace," Hume wrote, "is plain. It maintains that morality is determined by sentiment. It defines virtue to be whatever mental action or quality gives to a spectator the pleasing sentiment of approbation; and vice the contrary."[10] Such ideas find earlier precedents in the contention of the seventeenth-century scholar, Thomas Hobbes, that terms like good and evil simply reflected the relationship between things and people's passions.

> Whatsoever is the object of any man's appetite or desire, that is it which he for his art calleth *good:* and the object of his hate, and aversion, *evil*, and contemptible; and of his contempt, *vile* and *inconsiderable*. For these words of good, evil, and contemptible, are ever used with relation to the person that useth them: There being nothing simply and absolutely so; nor any common rule of good and evil, to be taken from the nature of the objects themselves.[11]

This combination of (1) a concern for utility (which Bentham defined as the degree of an action's conduciveness to the greater happiness of the greatest possible number of people in society), and (2) the definition of what is good according to the whims of human passions rather than of human reason, is at the heart of Bentham's thought. Hence, Bentham was highly sympathetic to the French Revolution's demolition of traditional laws, customs, and intermediate associations precisely because he viewed them as instances of "disutility." It would be an error to view Bentham as advocating changes in the social order because of a love of humanity. His protest was against the irrationality of disutility.

How, then, does Bentham arrive at the principle of utility as the basis reference point for not only assessing social institutions but for determining how we ought to act? In the first instance, Bentham simply dismisses any insights offered by metaphysics (without providing any substantive reason for doing so). Instead, he appeals to a naturalistic understanding of man. "Nature," Bentham claims, "has placed mankind under two masters, *pain* and pleasure . . . they govern us in all that we do, all that we say, in all that we think. . . . In words a man may pretend to abjure their empire, but in reality he will remain subject to it all the while."[12] It is difficult to detect much difference between this claim and Hume's maxim that reason is the slave of passions.

Bentham's statement about pain and pleasure is only a formal principle of morality; that is, it is a principle with no determinate content. Bentham simply asserts that people are moved to act primarily in order to experience pleasure and avoid pain. Bentham thus views the word "good" as a synonym for that which gives someone pleasure, while "evil" refers to the experience of pain. "On the one hand," he wrote, "the standard of right and wrong; on the other, the chain of cause and effect, are fastened to their [pleasure and pain's] throne."[13]

Pleasure and pain are the product of human action. In any given situation, Bentham observes, people may make a variety of choices concerning how they act. Presuming, however, that the good is pleasure and evil is pain, we may conclude that a "good" action is one that tends to increase the total sum of happiness (i.e., pleasure) while "evil" acts are those that reduce the sum of pleasure.

At this point, many philosophers begin to ask questions about the basic coherence of Bentham's position. His argument presumes that people can actually know all the possible effects of their actions and then decide—on the basis of a weighing of all the possible pleasures and pains proceeding from a variety of possible actions—which act is likely to produce the most pleasure.

Such a calculation is simply impossible. No one can make such an assessment without admitting a tremendous degree of ignorance about all the possible effects that might proceed from a freely chosen act. For if we purport to know—not "feel"—that one future embodies more good (pleasure) than any of its alternatives, then we are claiming to understand the future in a manner beyond the cognitive powers of human reason. Then there is the problem of "incommensurability": the inability to reduce all experiences and actions to one common measure in a way that meets the demands of reason. We cannot, for example, weigh pleasures and pains, because they have no common denominator. We cannot reasonably claim to be able to objectively measure, for example, the experience of unemployment, against growth in wisdom, against the death of a spouse, against a happy family.

As if aware of these objections, Bentham claimed that people could narrow the range of necessary calculations by making quantitative distinctions: that is, by suggesting that what brings more pleasure to people ought to be given greater weight than something that brings less pleasure. Here, however, Benthamite utilitarianism encounters further problems. Those who seek to engage in such a weighing are bound to narrow their focus. Yet, this reduction of horizons, as John Finnis explains, "cannot be guided by any *moral* principle of responsibility." Put differently, there is no morally objective criteria that can establish what is greater pleasure or lesser pain. This means that in the process of narrowing we will be guided primarily not by what we reason but, rather, by what we happen to want: in short, by what we desire rather than according to reason.[14]

We can, of course, attempt to introduce a measure such as numbers that reduce the different categories to a common denominator. This is precisely what Bentham (and Mill) did. He literally assigned numerical weights to various factors. This assignment of weights was, however, arbitrary. And it could not be anything else. For by what criteria does one assess one pleasure or pain as being greater than another? Benefits and harms in alternative actions must be commensurable if there is to be any reasonable judgment as to what is the lesser evil or greater good.

Ultimately, Bentham has to defer to the weight of public opinion. The ultimate content of the "greatest happiness" is thus left to be determined by the "greatest number."

The very notion of leaving the judgment of what is pleasurable and painful to majority opinion raises grave issues. If, for example, most of the population considered the destruction of a particular ethnic group to be the most pleasurable activity, Benthamite utilitarians would not, according to their theory, be able to object substantially to such an act.

Instead of addressing these obvious criticisms, Bentham sought to bolster the scientific claims of his theory by introducing a range of criteria—a type of hedonistic calculus[15]—by which individuals could assess the value of a pleasure or a pain. These included the intensity of a pleasure or pain; its duration; its likelihood; the degree of certainty or uncertainty that something will be pleasurable or painful; the purity or otherwise of the sensation; and the extent to which others are affected by the particular pain or pleasure. Again, however, no one can claim to have devised a manner of measuring the relative weight of these criteria against each other, precisely because of our inability to identify a common denominator that meets the demands of reason. Any such measurement cannot therefore claim to be rationally coherent.

Civilizing Bentham

To Mill's credit, he recognized many of these problems with Bentham's theory. Mill's response, however, was not to repudiate Bentham's concept of man's nature or Bentham's methodology. Despite his reservations, Mill largely agreed with Bentham's ideas, and praised Bentham for his quantitative approach to morality.[16]

Like Bentham, Mill's utilitarianism begins with the assertion—for it is no more than this—that the only phenomena that we can rightly assume that everyone experiences in common are the sensations of pleasure or pain. The desire to experience pleasure and avoid pain is, Mill holds, the only constant. Though people may claim to be seeking virtue for its own sake, Mill insists that "There was no original desire of it, or motive to it, save its conduciveness to pleasure; and especially to protection from pain."[17] Echoing Hume, Mill maintains that while reason can help us to determine the means of experiencing pleasure and avoiding pain, it cannot tell us if certain forms of pleasure or pain are in themselves reasonable or otherwise.

Mill is, however, anxious to avoid the charge of hedonistic egoism often leveled at Bentham's philosophy. Happiness ought not to be understood in egotistical terms, Mill holds, because happiness essentially concerns "the greatest amount of happiness altogether"[18] rather than that of a particular individual. Why the happiness of the group trumps that of the individual is not explained by Mill. Bentham himself vacillated his entire adult life about whether his utilitarianism sought to maximize the happiness of "everybody" or his own happiness.

Mill's next modification of Bentham's utilitarianism involves further simplification of the pain-pleasure calculus. People should adopt particular *rules*, Mill suggests, that deal with all cases of certain human acts, after assessing which rule best enhances pleasure and reduces pain for the greatest number. Stealing is forbidden, for example, because this rule increases the net aggregate of pleasure. In effect, Mill proposes that we move from a utilitarianism focused upon the pleasure and pain of actions, to a utilitarianism based upon calculation of the likely pleasure and pain produced by different rules.

Unfortunately for Mill, what is often called "rule-utilitarianism" does not simplify the calculations required in a reasonable manner. This becomes evident when we think about how such a rule is to be determined. The consistent rule-utilitarian can only know what rule will increase the aggregate sum of pleasure by (1) assessing each and every situation that could possibly arise with regard to a particular act, and then (2) deriving the most relevant rule from that calculation. In short, the process that determines the rule itself relies upon an impossible calculation. As Finnis remarks: "A genuinely consequentialist assessment of alternative possibilities could never end, and could begin anywhere."[19] This suggests that it should never begin at all.

To strengthen his case against such objections, Mill suggested that when it comes to "weighing" pleasure and pain, people ought to consider the quality of a pleasure rather than simply issues of quantity.[20] As if fearful of the cultural leveling that would ensue from a quantity measurement, Mill indicated that we ought to subscribe more weight to, for example, the refined pleasure of watching opera as opposed to the raw thrill of watching a boxing match.

At this point, Mill's utilitarianism becomes especially inconsistent with its own premises. The measure of utility in Mill's schema remains pleasure (even though Mill himself admitted that the ultimate sanction for the principle of utility is "a subjective feeling in our minds").[21] But if people are to distinguish one pleasure from another on the basis of quality, then another reference point is required. Hence, as the historian of philosophy Frederick Copleston famously observed, Mill is forced to resort to other standards than to pleasure itself.[22]

Mill justifies this by claiming that Bentham's view of human nature is excessively narrow. It reflects, Mill maintains, Bentham's failure to understand that man is a "being capable of pursuing spiritual perfection as an end; of desiring for its own sake, the conformity of his own character to his standard of excellence, without hope of good or fear of evil from other source than his own inward consciousness."[23]

In proceeding down this path, Mill appeals to ideas about human fulfillment that are irreconcilable with the priority of utility. It is impossible to explain why one experience should be regarded as "higher" than another simply by reference to pleasure. If the sole reference point remains pleasure, then the determination of quality has to be a purely subjective individual judgment. The only way to resolve this dilemma is either to admit that other criteria are equally applicable (and thereby deny the central principle of utilitarianism), or to appeal to majority preference concerning what is pleasurable.

Further complicating matters is that while Mill sought to nuance Bentham's hedonistic vision of man, Mill never established what he meant by "human nature." Certainly, Mill wanted to improve upon human nature. When describing that upon which he wants to improve, Mill refers to phenomena such as "individuality,"[24] the "higher faculties,"[25] or "the permanent interests of man as a progressive being."[26] Yet, as noble as these sentiments may seem, Mill at no stage defined what these "permanent interests" might be. Nor did Mill illustrate how such interests were integrated into his anthropology of man as a "progressive being" or explain what is "progressive."

It would only be possible for utilitarianism, be it of the "act" or "rule" type, to function as a coherent philosophical system if one of two conditions prevailed. The first condition would be if all human beings have some single well-defined goal (as opposed to something as vague as "pleasure") against which everything could be reasonably measured. Such a goal does not, however, exist. The number of life-plans that can be pursued by any one of us is literally incalculable. The second condition would be that if it were reasonable to hold that every single desire should prima facie be regarded as equally valid. This is, however, equally implausible. What possible *reason*, Finnis asks, could be given for treating the desire of someone who wants to remain ignorant as entitled to the same satisfaction as the desire of someone who wants to pursue knowledge?[27]

Utilitarians who depart from either of these conditions immediately involve themselves in contradiction. Mill, we recall, appeals to the advancement of individuality as a reason to defend his utilitarian vision of liberty. Nevertheless, as noted by the liberal philosopher Chandran Kukathas, "the immediate implication of this is that ways of life which do not value individuality cannot be accorded the same respect or protection as they uphold values which are at odds with the fundamental values of the liberal state."[28] Yet neither the utilitarian calculus nor utilitarian premises provide any reason why the flourishing of individuality should be given preference over the flourishing of a collective.

Perhaps the most disturbing implication of all utilitarian premises and rea-soning is that lurking beneath them is a logic incapable of resisting the claims of raw power. Once we accept the utilitarian vision of man as a creature constantly seeking pleasure and agree that it is right for him to pursue pleasure (however defined), we cannot in principle object to ourselves being viewed as objects to be used by others as instruments of their pleasure. Moreover, if we hold that the greatest pleasure of the greatest number must prevail, there is again nothing in principle to prevent a majority in a community from deciding that some mem-bers of the group may be used *solely* for the pleasure of others.

A standard utilitarian objection to this line of reasoning is that Mill's famous harm principle—that is, that our actions should be generally considered permis-sible provided they do not harm others—should prevent such situations from occurring. We cannot, however, on the one hand, appeal to the harm principle without conceding that humans are more than mere pleasure-calculators and enjoy a certain dignity that cannot be infringed upon. Once utilitarians do this, they effectively compromise their understanding of human persons. On the other hand, if they choose to stay within the utilitarian paradigm, they cannot explain why humans should not, as a matter of principle, be harmed. Nor can they iden-tify the source of the implicit dignity at the root of the inherent claim of protec-tion implicit to Mill's harm principle.

Utilitarianism and the Modern Mind

These criticisms of Mill and the utilitarian project are hardly new. They have been articulated in different forms by religious and secular thinkers alike. Benjamin Constant's *Journal Intime* may be read as one nineteenth-century lib-eral's parody of utilitarian calculation. In this text, the writer keeps adding and subtracting factors, measuring the pros and cons of each possible choice, adopt-ing each day a different option. He consequently experiences the sheer absurdity of such existential arithmetic, without ever reaching the desired result. In this deceptive algebra, in which not only every individual but every aspect of every individual is a separate universe, Constant illustrates that trying to measure the incommensurable is a problem that admits to no solution.[29]

Constant also recognized that utilitarianism's implications were not con-fined to reducing human life to incomprehensibility. He insisted that utilitarian-ism's apparent triumph in the aftermath of the French Revolution had contributed to murderous political strategies.[30] In Constant's vitriolic portrait of Napoleon, Bentham's utilitarianism incarnates itself not in the enlightened calculations of an efficiently benevolent Emperor Marcus Aurelius but, rather in the unscrupu-lous ambition and brutal effectiveness of the Corsican general who is presented as the archetype of the modern utilitarian ruler.[31] If the schemes of military con-quest pursued by Constant's Napoleon betray a type of archaic concept of political relations, his ruthless handling of power reflects a form of moral collapse that is essentially and menacingly modern.

Few philosophers today would explicitly identify themselves as Benthamite utilitarians. Yet, many appear unable to escape from resorting to some type of "calculus" of good and evil, or have proved powerless to avoid some reliance upon utility or preference when distinguishing between reasonable and unreasonable acts. For all its incoherence, utilitarian thinking has permeated so much contemporary thought that even some of its detractors have found themselves unable to escape its clutches. Two twentieth-century liberal examples of such critics are Friedrich von Hayek and John Rawls.

Hayek as Utilitarian

Among the formative influences upon Hayek's thought was his fellow Austrian free-market economist, Ludwig von Mises. Careful study of Mises' works soon reveals his utilitarian inclinations. In his most important book, *Human Action*, Mises maintains that what he calls the "liberal and democratic movement of the eighteenth and nineteenth century drew a great part of its strength from the doctrine of natural law."[32] Mises expresses, however, some impatience with this. He insists:

> The teachings of utilitarian philosophy and classical economics have nothing at all to do with the doctrine of natural right. With them the only point that matters is social utility. They recommend popular government, private property, tolerance, and freedom not because they are natural and just but because they are beneficial.[33]

Having highlighted the priority of utility, Mises proceeds to quote, approvingly, Bentham's insistence that the concept of natural rights is rhetorical nonsense and then reminds his reader that utilitarians "do not combat arbitrary government and privileges because they are against natural law but because they are detrimental to prosperity."[34]

As an economist unafraid to engage in philosophical reflection, Hayek was always conscious of the implicit reliance upon utility underlying Mises' positions. It was, however, only later in life that Hayek, by his own account, was "led, by a very painful process, gradually to reject what in my youth I regarded as the latest insight, and what even my great master, Ludwig von Mises, made the basis of his philosophy: the utilitarian explanation of ethics."[35] Hayek's primary reason for his reluctant repudiation was his conclusion that utilitarianism is a profoundly rationalistic doctrine—"the idea that we have the intellectual power to arrange everything rationally."[36] Utilitarianism thus inclined people to believe that States and economies can be planned. This leads to socialism. Not surprisingly, this deduction led Hayek, as a convinced anti-Socialist, to reject utilitarianism.

In the second volume of his legal treatise, *Law, Legislation and Liberty*, Hayek underlines the impossibility of the Benthamite utilitarian calculus by noting that it "presupposes that all the particular individual effects of any one action can be known by the acting person."[37] "Act-utilitarianism" demands full knowledge of the consequences of a particular act. This, Hayek recognizes, makes impossible demands upon any individual due to our inability to foresee all the effects of any one of our actions. Hayek is equally critical of "rule-utilitarianism." This fails, he argues, because it presupposes that other rules are "taken as given and generally observed and not determined by any known utility." In other words, the rule-utilitarian assumes that certain traditions will persist even though they may be unexplainable in utility terms. Hence, Hayek contends that, "among the determinants of the utility of any one rule there would always be other rules which could not be justified by their utility."[38]

Despite rejecting act- and rule-utilitarianism, Hayek remained profoundly influenced by utilitarian concepts and methodology. Only a few pages after writing the foregoing words, Hayek comments that "[t]he essence of all rules of conduct is that they label kinds of actions, not in terms of their largely unknown effects in particular instances but in terms of their probable effects which need not be foreseeable by the individuals."[39]

The first question arising from this statement concerns how can we know that the effects of an action are probable if they are not foreseeable by individuals? But, more importantly, Hayek's statement implies all laws of behavior should be based upon their probable effects. Thus there *does* seem to be a form of rule-utilitarianism at work in Hayek's thought. The difference between Hayek and Mill is that Mill has more confidence in man's capacity to design such rules consciously. Hayek is therefore a type of indirect rule-utilitarian, who prefers to see such rules evolve over time. While it is true that Hayek rejects the rationalistic dimension of utilitarianism, he does believe that rules should be determined (in an evolutionary manner) by an assessment of their effects.

This is not the only evidence of utilitarian influences upon Hayek's thinking. The social order outlined in his 1960 book, *The Constitution of Liberty*, for example, is defended as likely to facilitate a system in which the poor are most likely to see improvement in their material well-being.[40] Similarly, Hayek's confidence in freedom is based on "the belief that it will, on balance, release more forces for the good than for the bad."[41] Even in the course of critiquing utilitarianism, Hayek states that "[W]e may of course aim at 'the greatest happiness of the greatest number'"[42]—a sentiment that places Hayek squarely in the camp of Bentham and Mill.

Rawls as Utilitarian

The political theorist John Rawls is another contemporary liberal who sought to disassociate his thought from the utilitarianism of Bentham and Mill. In his profoundly influential book, *A Theory of Justice*, Rawls states that critics of

Bentham and Mill have "pointed out the obscurities of the principle of utility and noted the apparent incongruities between many of its implications and our moral sentiments."[43] Rawls is concerned, for example, about "the vagueness in the idea of average (or total) well-being." He also recognizes that the problems involved in arriving at "an estimate of utility functions" are "so great and the approximations are so rough that deeply conflicting opinions may seem equally plausible to different persons."[44]

At the same time, Rawls believes that critics of utilitarianism have "failed to construct a workable and systematic moral concept to oppose it."[45] Hence, Rawls attempts "to work out a theory of justice that represents an alternative to utilitarian thought generally and so to all . . . general versions of it."[46] His theory is certainly complex, but it needs to be outlined so as to illustrate Rawls' own failure to escape the utilitarian paradigm.

Like many liberals, Rawls is anxious to find procedures that allow contemporary societies to live peacefully and justly despite the fact of profound internal disagreement over fundamental issues. Significantly, Rawls' interest in identifying such procedures and principles is not to establish what people ought to want to do. He is more concerned with creating a situation whereby every person is able to pursue what he desires, consistent with the freedom of others to pursue what they desire.

To achieve his aim, Rawls attempts to derive principles of justice from what he views as the most uncontroversial assumptions that everyone, regardless of their faith, politics, or life-experience, can agree upon, be they a devout Muslim or a passionate secularist. This standpoint, which he calls the "Original Position," is fixed by the following four principles:

1. Everyone in the original position must determine, by unanimous agreement, the principles of justice for any and every society in which they might live.

2. In settling these principles, everyone in the original position is concerned to guarantee that, in whatever society we find ourselves in real life, we will have as much of what Rawls calls the "primary goods" (defined as self-respect, liberty, opportunity, and wealth) as we can secure by agreeing to these principles.

3. Everyone comes to this agreement behind a "veil of ignorance." Put simply, we do not know what society we will live in. Nor do we know what will be our status, natural assets, psychology, or concepts of the good in that society.

4. In reaching agreement on the principles of justice, each party in the original position is not particularly concerned about the interests of others. They are not benevolent, egotistic, or envious. They have no ethical motivations and, above all, no concept of anything being intrinsically good.

(Curiously, Rawls maintains this view despite acknowledging that, in the real world, human reason *can* identify what
are basic values and their opposites.)[47]

There are two main principles that, Rawls argues, all parties would agree
upon in the original position, and which therefore qualify as principles of justice.
The first is that each person must have "an equal right to the *most extensive total
system* of equal basic liberties with a similar system of liberty for all."[48] Any person, Rawls holds, in the original position would choose the principle of equal
liberty because he would consider it imprudent to gamble away his own future
liberty by acknowledging principles that, in real life, would allow others to
restrict his freedom to pursue whatever plan of life he desires.

Here one is bound to ask Rawls: How are we to determine the "extent" of a
"total system" of liberties, given that many freedoms, such as freedom from invasion of privacy and freedom of press investigation, are incommensurable?[49] No
one can plausibly claim, for instance, that so much freedom of expression is
worth less or more than so much freedom of inquiry. Implicit therefore to Rawls'
thinking is the utilitarian presumption that these liberties can be weighed against
other freedoms. And thus, Rawls commits the utilitarian methodological error of
imagining that the immeasurable can be measured.

The second principle that Rawls derives from his original position is also
characterized by implicit utilitarian influences. Rawls calls this axiom the "difference principle": The arrangement of social and economic institutions—in particular, social and economic inequalities—must always be to the advantage (in
the sense of Rawls' "primary goods") of the least advantaged class. Rawls arrives
at this conclusion on three grounds. First, no one in the original position would
risk being abandoned at the bottom of the social heap. Second, the least advantaged in any social order might rebel against any principle other than this. Third,
no one in the original position uses concepts of worth; the veil of ignorance forbids people referring to any concept of the good. They therefore would never
agree that the question of how we distribute things should take criteria of merit
or worthiness into account.

In Rawls' world, the "difference principle" means that whatever arrangement is decided upon, it must benefit the least advantaged. But how do we determine who is the least advantaged in any one situation? Once—as Rawls insists
that we must—considerations such as merit and worthiness are excluded, we
cannot look backwards to judge who, for example, has worked harder or contributed more. We are thus forced to make an *arbitrary* judgment about when to
assess the validity of the precise distribution of goods at any one point of time in
the future.

Here, again, we discover a method of reasoning deeply influenced by utilitarianism. For utilitarianism relies upon the arbitrary selection of a single future
moment as the point at which "all" the consequences of some proposed act will

be assessed. The selection of this time cannot be anything but arbitrary, yet it is implicit to the utilitarian calculus proposed by both Bentham and Mill. To the extent that Rawls relies upon such arbitrariness, he remains ensnared by utilitarianism and fails to achieve his goal of constructing a reasonable alternative.

A Return to the Person

The examples of Hayek and Rawls illustrate the extent to which modern critics of utilitarianism have been powerfully shaped by a philosophy they repudiate. Other contemporary theorists, such as the political philosopher John Gray, explicitly reject Mill's claim to have devised a way of measuring human happiness. Gray subsequently urges a return to the following of tradition. Gray does not hold this view because he considers tradition to embody truth but, rather, because he believes that the accumulated behavior of the past provides us with the safest way to navigate our path through the future[50]—a position remarkably similar to the thinking underlying Hayek's indirect rule-utilitarianism.

An immensely practical problem, however, with Gray's response is the increasing difficulty of identifying a tradition that all people in, for example, Western democracies will happily identify. More seriously, Gray evidently believes that reason cannot lead us to know some type of universal standard of reasonable action—a central claim of David Hume's thought. To this extent, Gray remains firmly within the fold of Humean skepticism.

At the root of utilitarianism is widespread acceptance of Hume's axiom about reason and the passions. What is "good" and "evil" for Hume (and Bentham) is a question of sentiment and utility rather than which acts present themselves to man's reason as good or evil. Those who seek an intellectually coherent alternative to utilitarianism as a basis for a free political order therefore need to illustrate (1) how reason, properly situated within the totality of the human person, allows us to discern the appropriate ends of human acts, (2) why it is reasonable to want to choose such acts, and (3) the implications of this for the political order.

There is, however, another reason for articulating a sound philosophy of liberty and the free society based upon real, existing man. In a relatively unknown essay entitled "German Nihilism," penned in the dark days of 1941, the philosopher Leo Strauss warned that a society's discarding of utilitarianism might lead to something even worse if a sound concept of man did not replace it. The rejection of utilitarianism by many nineteenth-century German scholars, Strauss claimed, had led to flirtations with romanticism, nationalism, and militarism as people sought to perform courageous acts, having concluded that courage was the only unambiguous value in a world of uncertainty.[51] This naked will to self-assertiveness had, for Strauss, achieved its apotheosis in the nightmare of Nazism.

Courage in itself is insufficient. Many have shown great courage while fighting to crush freedom. To see the unreasonableness of utilitarianism replaced by brave existential acts will be of no service to liberty. Only a return to the human person in his totality will allow freedom's full meaning for man to become apparent to man.

Notes

1. Tocqueville, *Democracy*, vol. 2, 461.

2. John Henry Newman, *The Letters and Diaries of John Henry Newman*, ed. C. D. Dessain, vol. 2 (Oxford: Oxford University Press, 1978–1984), 130.

3. Ibid., ed. C. S. Dessain et al., vol. 28 (Oxford: Clarendon Press, 1973–1977), 196.

4. Ibid., vol. 29, 200.

5. See John Henry Newman, *Loss and Gain: The Story of a Convert* (Oxford: Oxford University Press, 1986), 69.

6. George, *Making Men Moral*, 75.

7. See Frederick Copleston, S.J., *A History of Philosophy*, bk. 2, vol. 6 (New York: Image Books, 1985), 35–38.

8. Jeremy Bentham, *A Fragment on Government*, ed. Wilfrid Harrison (Oxford: Basil Blackwell, 1948).

9. David Hume, *An Enquiry Concerning the Principles of Morals*, ed. Tom L. Beauchamp (Oxford: Clarendon Press, 1998), 145.

10. Ibid., 129.

11. Thomas Hobbes, *Leviathan* (Harmondsworth: Penguin, 1968), c. 6.

12. Bentham, *Introduction to the Principles of Morals and Legislation*, c. 1, sec. 1.

13. Bentham, *Introduction*, chap. 1, sec. 1.

14. See John Finnis, *Moral Absolutes: Tradition, Revision, and Truth* (Washington, D.C.: Catholic University of America Press, 1991), 18.

15. See Bentham, *Introduction*, chap. 1, sec. 3.

16. Mill, *Dissertations and Discussions*, 339–40.

17. John Stuart Mill, *Utilitarianism and Other Writings*, ed. M. Warnock (New York: Meridian, 1962), 56–57.

18. Mill, *Utilitarianism*, 16.

19. Finnis, *Natural Law*, 117.

20. See Mill, *Utilitarianism*, 11–12.

21. Mill, *Utilitarianism*, 281.

22. Frederick Copleston, S.J., *A History of Philosophy*, vol. 8, bk. 3 (New York: Image Books, 1985), 30–31.

23. Mill, *On Liberty*, 9.

24. Ibid., 56.

25. Mill, *Utilitarianism*, 16.

26. Mill, *On Liberty*, 9.

27. See Finnis, *Natural Law*, 113.

28. Chandran Kukathas, *Hayek and Modern Liberalism* (Oxford: Clarendon Press, 1989), 255.

29. Benjamin Constant, *Oeuvres*, ed. A. Roulin (Paris: Cerf, 1957), 36.

30. See Benjamin Constant, *De la religion considerée dans sa source, ses formes et ses développements*, vol. 1 (Paris: Gaillot, 1935), 29–30.

31. See Benjamin Constant, *The Political Writings of Benjamin Constant*, ed. Biancamaria Fontana (Cambridge: Cambridge University Press, 1988), 56–59, 79–81.

32. Ludwig von Mises, *Human Action: A Treatise on Economics*, 3d rev. ed. (Chicago: Henry Regnery Company, 1966), 174.

33. Mises, *Human Action*, 175.

34. Ibid.

35. Friedrich Hayek, *Knowledge, Evolution and Society* (London: Adam Smith Institute, 1983), 46.

36. Friedrich Hayek, *Hayek on Hayek: An Autobiographical Dialogue*, ed. S. Kresge and Leif Wenar (Chicago: University of Chicago Press, 1994), 73.

37. Friedrich Hayek, *Law, Legislation and Liberty*, vol. 2, *The Mirage of Social Justice* (Chicago: University of Chicago Press, 1976), 19.

38. Hayek, *Mirage of Social Justice*, 20.

39. Ibid., 22.

40. See Hayek, *Constitution*, 44.

41. Ibid., 31.

42. Hayek, *Mirage of Social Justice*, 23.

43. John Rawls, *A Theory of Justice* (Harvard: Harvard University Press, 1971), viii.

44. Ibid., 320.

45. Ibid., viii.

46. Ibid., 22.

47. Ibid., 328.

48. Ibid., 250 (emphasis added).

49. See H. L. A. Hart, "Rawls on Liberty and its Priority," *University of Chicago Law Review*, 40 (1973): 534.

50. See John Gray, *Liberalisms: Essays in Political Philosophy* (London: Routledge and Kegan Paul, 1989), 236.

51. Leo Strauss, "German Nihilism," *Interpretation: A Journal of Political Philosophy*, 26, no. 3 (1999): 353–78.

3

The Drama of Human Freedom

They should use their liberty with discretion.

—Livy[1]

Man, it would seem, is destined to want to be free. From the dawn of civilization, the word *freedom* has resonated in texts ranging from the tales of Homer to the writings of Marx. Liberty is a centerpiece of the claims of the Christian Gospel, the Glorious Revolution of 1688, the Americans who rose against George III, as well as of the events of 1789.

In the midst of these struggles, discussion of the nature of freedom has been characterized by profound disagreement, especially in terms of liberty's implications for the social order. One of the most famous eighteenth-century French constitutionalists, Charles de Montesquieu, believed that liberty "consists in security or in one's opinion of one's security."[2] By contrast, the early nineteenth-century German philosopher G. W. F. Hegel portrayed freedom as being achieved through the paradox of everyone's mutual submission to the State, an entity that he accorded a type of quasi-divine status.[3]

Such debates are more than the stuff of abstract speculation. They have profound implications for real flesh-and-blood human beings. What, we ask, is so special about liberty that people would be willing to uproot entire political systems to achieve it? Why would people be willing to die rather than endure unjust coercion? Why, in short, *should* man be free? Why is it *worth* being free? Are we to live just for agreeable experiences? Is this really the summation of our liberty?

Complicating matters are the many who question the very possibility of freedom. Particularly since the time of the French Enlightenment *philosophe* Jean-Jacques Rousseau, many intellectual disciplines have stressed the psychological urges, cultural factors, social influences, and economic conditions affecting an individual's potential to choose. Enhanced knowledge of these conditions has certainly helped many societies to be more attentive to the impact of such factors upon human choice. This, however, must be balanced against the fact that many working in the behavioral sciences have largely concluded that reason only allows us to decide *how* we achieve certain objectives—the ends being the result not of reasoned choice but the unfathomable and therefore unchosen workings of our emotions, which themselves are often reduced to the workings of chemical processes within man or to the results of each person's particular cultural conditioning. Ironically, many of the very same people working in these areas will not hesitate to tell others, such as those formulating public policy, what they morally ought or ought not to do. They fail to realize that the discernment of moral oughts and prohibitions simply cannot be determined by the empirical methodology of the natural and behavioral sciences. The fact that we know how, for example, to clone an animal does not provide us with any morally decisive information concerning whether we should do so.

These developments reflect what can only be described as a crisis of truth. Natural science has encouraged a skepticism concerning anything that cannot be explained or proven by its methods such as formal empirical observation. Anything else, especially claims of moral truth, is often deemed to be a subjective interpretation and therefore not universally binding. Thus, the study of philosophy, for example, has been reduced in many cases to language games that result in the endless categorization and recategorization of expressions and phrases, a process that strenuously avoids attachment of any concept of good or evil to the very same words and terms.

Reinforcing these tendencies has been awareness that many opinions have claimed the title of truth and, in the name of truth, suppressed freedom and murdered millions, be it by guillotine, gas chamber, or gulag. This latter concern was at the heart of the famous essay, "Two Concepts of Liberty," by the British liberal theorist, Sir Isaiah Berlin.

According to Berlin, one concept of freedom is "negative liberty." This involves not being interfered with by others: The less others interfere with my choices, the greater my freedom.[4] Negative liberty thus signifies the extent to which the political order is not coercive. It seeks to guarantee the greatest possible domain for choice, especially by resisting any truth-claim that might limit choice.

Berlin's second concept of freedom, "positive liberty," is by contrast defined as "the liberty to." More specifically, Berlin had in mind the freedom to realize one's true self, often in terms of our identity as a member of a tribe, race, Church, or State; or the freedom to actualize some superior end in history.

Any perusal of Berlin's essay soon reveals his conviction that within positive freedom there lurks a totalitarian impulse, for once someone claims to know what people ought to do, the temptation is to force others also to realize their true self, and thus "ignore the actual wishes of men or societies, to bully, oppress, torture them in the name, and on behalf, of their 'real' self."[5] The claim to be pursuing positive freedom, Berlin argued, all too easily degenerated into a justification for tyranny.

This uneasiness about the possible implications of commitments to positive liberty reflects Berlin's very twentieth-century attentiveness to the crippling effects upon freedom of totalitarianism, be it Communist or Fascist in nature. Yet it may be that Berlin neglected the danger to free societies posed by negative liberty's wariness about truth-claims. The philosopher Richard Rorty has claimed that only on the basis of relativism is democracy safe. "No specific doctrine," he writes, "is much of a danger, but the idea that democracy depends on adhesion to some such doctrine is."[6] In place of truth, Rorty proposes "a cheerful nihilism" which holds that we should politely disdain any claim to truth independent of pragmatic social preference. In Rorty's view, the search for impartial standards against which humans can judge themselves is futile. Nonetheless, Rorty adds, those who hold to no objective standard and claim no foundation in practical reason can still feel outrage about unjust curtailments of liberty.[7]

But how, one must ask, are we to discern the *truth* of such emotions? How can we *know* that they are indeed just without the type of reference point that Rorty rejects? Nor can we fail to note that people holding Rorty's views need not feel any obligation to oppose tyranny. As a matter of principle, they do not lose anything by quietly adapting to a suppression of freedom. For them, there is no standard suggesting that they ought to resist such developments.

In fact, without truth claims, there is *nothing* to which we can morally appeal in order to defend freedom. If there is only opinion—your opinion, my opinion, everyone else's opinion—but no truth, and if every opinion is valid simply by virtue of being freely chosen, then we could state: "The Nazis cannot be held accountable for their choices because they acted according to their own preferences, they showed real commitment to their opinions; and who in any case is to judge that what they did was wrong?" In such an atmosphere, public debate ceases to be a matter of reasoned discussion of the truth of people's opinions. Instead, politics is reduced to a question of who can provide their opinion with legislative weight. Truth, it seems, may not be as great a threat to liberty as Berlin supposes. Absence of truth, however, certainly is.

Berlin's wariness about introducing the notion of truth into any discussion of freedom mirrors other liberal philosophers' reflections about liberty. Hayek spent most of his life thinking about how to promote a social order grounded in freedom. Like Berlin, he was profoundly influenced by the crisis of liberal order that eventually condemned much of twentieth-century Europe to authoritarian rule. It led Hayek to attempt a rearticulation of a classical liberal vision of liberty capable of resisting any slide into despotism, but for all its strengths, his theory

remains imprisoned by an inability to explain coherently the relationship between
reason and free choice.

Liberty, Coercion, and Progress

Hayek's most succinct treatment of freedom is found in his 1960 text, *The
Constitution of Liberty*. Though this book was largely ignored by most scholars
at its time of publication, there is little question that many who describe themselves (despite the terrible ambiguity of the term) as "classical liberals," regard
The Constitution of Liberty as a much needed restatement of their political vision.

In broad terms, the vision of freedom articulated in *The Constitution of
Liberty* is most analogous to Berlin's negative liberty. The state of liberty, Hayek
states, is "that condition of men in which coercion of some by others is reduced
as much as possible in society."[8] Hayek then explains why this is the essence of
freedom by comparing it with other understandings of liberty. He distinguishes it
from, for example, "political freedom."[9] This concerns the participation of people in government. Quite correctly, Hayek observes that this does not mean that
coercion will be reduced to a minimum.

Another idea that Hayek considers is "that of 'inner' or 'metaphysical' . . .
freedom." Defining this "as the extent to which a person is guided in his actions
by his own considered will, by his reason or lasting conviction, rather than by
momentary impulse or circumstance," Hayek believes that inner freedom dis-
tracts our attention from the essence of freedom from coercion. For the opposite
of inner freedom, according to Hayek, is "not coercion by others but the influence of temporary emotions, or moral or intellectual weakness." He then adds,
"Whether or not a person is able to choose intelligently between alternatives, or
to adhere to a resolution he has made, is a problem distinct from whether or not
other people will impose their will upon him."[10] Certainly, Hayek is prepared to
agree that, taken together, "inner freedom" and "freedom from coercion" determine how much use a person makes of his opportunities. Nonetheless, Hayek is
distinctly uncomfortable with the idea, which he describes as a "sophism," "that
we are free only if we do what in some sense we ought to do."[11]

At no point does Hayek explain why he believes that "freedom to do as we
ought" is a fallacious notion. We can only speculate. If Hayek means that we
should be wary of those who insist that unless we obey them, we will never be
free, then Hayek is right. Such thinking lies at the heart of Hegel's apotheosis of
the State.

There is, however, another possibility: that Hayek is dismissing the idea of
freedom as the self-mastery that we achieve when we act in accordance with the
concrete state in which we receive our freedom. If so, then Hayek's argument is
open to serious question. This becomes clear when we ask the following question. "Are we, as embodied persons, truly free if we view ourselves as a dog, a
slave, or a plant?" The answer is surely a resounding no, for this amounts to a

view of choice as somehow "liberated" not only from reason, but the truth about our humanness: that is, reality.

It is this logical fallacy that lies at the heart of the United States Supreme Court's 1992 definition of liberty "as the right to define one's own concept of existence, of being, of the universe, and of the mystery of human life."[12] Certainly as the sixteenth-century Christian humanist, jurist, and martyr Sir Thomas More wrote, we have the capacity as rational creatures to concoct many "worldly fantasies" of our own making.[13] We can always rebel against the inclinations of our reason. This, however, only leads us to neglect what is reasonable and true—and therefore reality—and enter into the untruth of escapism. In More's words, "Is it not a beastly thing to see a man that has reason so rule himself that his feet may not bear him, but . . . rolls and reels until he falls into the gutter?"[14] Such people are not free: They are simply swept wherever the current takes them, a slave of unreality and self-delusion.

The same problem can be highlighted by asking another question: Why does Hayek believe that it is important for man to be free from coercion? To this query, Hayek has two responses.

One is that coercion makes one person the instrument of a second person's will, not for the first person's sake but for the purpose of the coercer.[15] Hayek thus appears to regard coercion as representing an affront to each person as a thinking individual who should be valued for his own sake.

Hayek's primary concern about coercion, however, is that civilizational progress is radically dependent on individual freedom. Progress, Hayek maintains, does not normally occur as a result of people's seeking to resolve problems in a coerced or collective manner. Progress comes when individuals freely act upon their particular knowledge of their unique circumstances and abilities in the course of pursuing their own chosen purposes. It is precisely because one person cannot know everything, Hayek maintains, that we should place our trust in the independent and sometimes competitive acts of many people, and allow this process to determine what is worth keeping or discarding.[16] Hayek's faith in freedom therefore "does not rest on the foreseeable results in particular circumstances but on the belief that it will, on balance, release more forces for the good than for the bad."[17] His justification for minimizing coercion is therefore somewhat utilitarian.

That Hayek makes an important point about the character of material and cultural development is not in question. Our knowledge of real, existing Communism reminds us that collectivism invariably leads to economic stagnation, political repression, and widespread corruption.

Leaving aside the difficulties with the utilitarian basis for Hayek's defense of liberty as essential for progress, we should note that Hayek has surprisingly little to say about the *content* of progress. He even concedes that progress "in the sense of the cumulative growth of knowledge and power over nature is a term that says little about whether the new state will give us more satisfaction than the old." Such a question, Hayek comments, is "probably unanswerable."[18] For

Hayek, however, this does not matter. More important is "successful striving for what at each moment seems attainable," or "movement for movement's sake."[19]

This response leaves unanswered some very important questions: Toward what are people moving? What are they becoming in the process of doing so? In many responses to such queries, one can almost detect the sneer of the devil Mephistopheles in Goethe's play *Faust:* "The future creates what is moral." From Hayek's perspective, it is enough that progress enables larger numbers of people to derive pleasure from their existence, be it through striving for particular objectives or enjoying the material benefits of progress.[20]

Yet, while no one wishes to experience dullness and melancholy, pleasurable sensations cannot be reasonably equated with fulfillment. Such explanations only take into account one aspect of human existence. This may be illustrated by the example of a person who derives much pleasure from consuming poisoned food and then dies as a consequence. However enjoyable may have been that person's state of consciousness while eating the food, one can hardly conclude that the experience was fulfilling for the person.[21]

Human fulfillment is much more than the experience of pleasure and avoidance of pain. Acceptance of this proposition is, however, closely associated with recognizing that man can, in light of his reason, freely choose good and avoid evil. Hayek himself is somewhat skeptical of man's capacity to engage in this type of reasoning. Instead, he articulates a type of evolutionary understanding of morality and approvingly quotes David Hume to the effect that "the rules of morality are not the conclusions of our reason."[22]

Like Hume, Hayek tends to view morality as a type of spontaneous conformity to the mores and habits that a civilization has developed. Hayek therefore insists that these mores and rules are not divinely ordained, an integral part of human nature, or revealed by right reason. Rather, they result from human experience and the utility contributed by each habit and rule to human welfare. Thus, we are simply born into a system of values and this supplies the ends that our reason must serve.[23] Ultimately, Hayek suggests, the survival of mores depends on their ability to facilitate progress.[24]

These statements remind us just how deeply Hayek shares in that tradition of skepticism perhaps most associated with Hume. Hayek himself actually conceded "that in some respects the liberal is fundamentally a skeptic."[25] Hence, we should not be surprised that Hayek dismisses the idea of freedom as self-mastery as a sophisticated fiction, for his arguments, like Hume's, rely heavily upon our acceptance of a subjectivist anthropology of man—an anthropology that is ultimately self-refuting.

The Specter of Skepticism

Since the last quarter of the twentieth century, it has been common to speak of a crisis of truth following the proliferation of those radically subjectivist theories often labeled "postmodern." This tendency disguises the fact that doubts about man's capacity to *know* have always existed. In the Greek world, Aristotle's *Ethics* wrestled, for example, with the skeptical relativism of the philosopher Aristippus.[26] It cannot, however, be denied that skepticism developed some of its strongest expressions in the post-Enlightenment period. In the words of the theologian Cardinal Joseph Ratzinger: "The modern attitude toward truth is summed up most succinctly in Pilate's question, 'What is truth?'"[27]

Following the various European Enlightenments of the seventeenth and eighteenth centuries, skepticism found new forms of philosophical expression, ranging from Hume's conservative tendency to Friedrich Nietzsche's apocalyptic variant.[28] These developments particularly worried a number of nineteenth-century liberals. Alexis de Tocqueville, for instance, described skepticism as an intellectual disposition that could only facilitate civilizational decline.[29]

The focus of skepticism, at least as posited by its most formidable proponents, Hobbes and Hume, is upon the nature of reason. Neither Hobbes nor Hume deny that man possesses reason. They simply insist that it is instrumental in character. Hobbes insisted, "The Thoughts are to the Desires as Scouts and Spies to range abroad, and find a way to the things desired."[30] If Hobbes and Hume are right, then it is impossible for people to know the proper ends of human choice through reason. Such ends do not therefore exist for man.

Philosophical skeptics invariably begin outlining their position by pointing to the persistent disagreement about philosophical, religious, and moral questions that exists within any given society. This, they suggest, indicates that man cannot arrive at a universal consensus about what is right, except for the type of consensus determined by dominant opinion (sometimes under the guise of tradition and convention). It is therefore reasonable, the skeptic suggests, to doubt any claim to know the truth, and to maintain that all choices are morally indifferent. On this basis, skeptics seriously doubt that human beings can make choices that are not, such as with animals, ultimately based upon the prompting of their instincts.

This is not to suggest that skepticism denies that there is any point to man seeking to be rational. The question is, rather, what do we mean by "rational"? Ratzinger maintains that the skeptic's "criterion of rationality is drawn solely from the experience of technological production on a scientific basis. Rationality is conceived in the direction of functionality, efficiency."[31] The solitary standard of rationality in this paradigm is therefore the technical possibility of acting. Possibility as such thus becomes a legitimate basis sufficient in itself for acting. Man may legitimately do whatever he is capable of doing.

The greatest strength of skepticism is its determination that humans do not deceive themselves into imagining that they can know everything: the error that invariably lies at the root of utopian propositions. To this extent, skeptics are concerned that man should be a reasonable creature.

At this point, however, skepticism becomes a self-refuting proposition, and if a basic principle of logic is that self-contradictory theses should be discarded, then skepticism should have been dispensed with long ago. The concern to be reasonable and avoid self-deception is the starting point of the philosophical quest for truth—the very pursuit that skeptics believe that man is incapable of. We may also ask: What reason could the skeptic have for desiring to comprehend that in the final analysis all is unknowable, *unless* he is caught up in a quest for truth? In other words, the skeptic draws his deduction that we should be skeptical about everything from foundational assumptions that he cannot doubt.

For the skeptic, reason is purely instrumental. Yet, in defending this position, the skeptic's reason necessarily engages in a noninstrumental task. He is presuming that it is *good* to *know* the *truth* of skepticism, and on grounds of reason rather than of feelings. As John Finnis remarks: "The reasonableness of taking such claims seriously and of treating them as giving one a reason to spend time reflecting on their content is inconsistent with their content."[32]

If this is true, then it is inconsistent for skeptics to assert that all viewpoints are simply a matter of arbitrary opinion. When the skeptic posits that humans can only be motivated by sentiment rather than by reason, he is not proposing this statement as his own impulsive preference. He is portraying it as a *reasonable* statement; that is, he is making the rational judgment that any claim about human action cannot be based on reason. The skeptic makes no claim that he simply feels that emotions are the only starting point for human acts. Even to arrive at this conclusion or to defend it requires reasoned reflection. The conservative nineteenth-century philosopher Joseph de Maistre underscored the irony of this when observing that it was through reason that Enlightenment skeptics had sought to banish reason![33]

As for the skeptic's attention to the fact of disagreement, this does not prove the "unknowability" of anything beyond the power of natural science. Over 700 years ago, Aquinas pointed out that disagreement often results from people making errors as they reason their way toward possible choices. A diversity of views may also reflect the significant room for legitimate prudential judgment that exists with regard to the reasonable answers that people can give to many questions. Some of these judgments may be incompatible with each other even though they are derived from the same principles. Then there are those cultural traditions and prejudices[34] that embody popular habits of succumbing to particular passions, and which blind people to what is reasonable. Nor, lastly, should we underestimate our capacity to act on the basis of passion and then to deploy our reason to rationalize unreasonable actions.

At this point, some might wonder: "What is the relevance of this relatively abstract philosophical argument for liberty? Does it really matter what position I take on this issue?"

The short answer to such queries is a definite yes. The implications of this debate are, as de Tocqueville understood, profound for human civilization.

Skepticism's relative success in permeating the modern outlook has resulted in a widespread consensus that reason is essentially technical in nature. In one sense, this is comprehensible. All around us, we see the extraordinary power of instrumental reason. It has put a man on the moon while also allowing us to see DNA, the very stuff that determines so much of who we are.

Unfortunately, instrumental reason cannot tell us what are reasonable uses of the products it creates. Technical efficiency in itself cannot tell us how to act. This is surely one of the harsher lessons of the twentieth century. While it was a period of great medical and scientific achievement, these years were also a century of moral catastrophe. The scientific reason that produced technological marvels proved incapable of providing us with the wisdom to know how to use it in ways that served rather than destroyed man. Without such wisdom, the products of instrumental reason can be easily turned against man himself in order to enslave him and ultimately destroy his freedom.

Herein lies the other threat of philosophical skepticism: It actively undermines liberty. This much becomes clear when we reflect upon Karl Marx's understanding of freedom. In his future Communist society, it would be possible "to do one thing today and another tomorrow; to hunt in the morning, fish in the afternoon, breed cattle in the evening, and criticize after dinner, just as I please."[35] Marx thus portrayed freedom as the right to do whatever we wish and to refrain from anything we do not wish to do. Each individual's will was to become the only principle of action.

The error pervading Marx's thought is its exclusion of any reference to reason. For how free is our will if we do not reason in a noninstrumental way about the choices that we make? To cite Ratzinger:

> Is an unreasonable will truly a free will? Is an unreasonable freedom truly freedom? Is it really a good? In order to prevent the tyranny of unreason must we not complete the definition of freedom as the capacity to will and to do what we will by placing it in the context of reason, of the totality of man? And will not the interplay between reason and will also involve the search for the common reason shared by all men and thus for the compatibility of liberties?[36]

These words point to an even more basic truth. If reason cannot tell us *what* to want but only *how* to attain whatever we happen to desire, then modern conceptual underpinnings of liberty such as human rights are undermined. For if rights are ultimately grounded in people's ever-shifting preferences, they lose all the absoluteness that the word "rights" entails and become subject to arbitrary opinion. In such circumstances, inalienable rights would no longer exist.

Another direct effect of the prevalence of skepticism is that choice becomes its own justification. It becomes impossible to speak of the reasonableness or otherwise of different choices, and therefore even the possibility of free choice, for unless we acknowledge that reason can judge the worth of certain actions— that it can discern the reasonableness of particular desires—and, on the basis of that judgment, direct us to choose one act instead of another, then we cannot say that our actions have been freely chosen. Instead, human acts can only be regarded as resulting either from external pressures, as posited by, for example, the "hard determinism" of Marx, or internal factors, such as whatever desire happens to be haphazardly surging through our consciousness at any one time. For all his extolling of liberty, Mill's writings reveal him to be essentially a "soft determinist." This is apparent from his distinction between two types of choices: those that were "free" in the sense that they came about necessarily but without coercion; and those that were "unfree" because they were coerced.[37]

Growing awareness of man's capacity to think himself into denying free choice should lead us to greater appreciation of Cardinal Jean-Marie Lustiger's observation that "reason has to learn wisdom."[38] Central to this educative process is man's need to rediscover the truth about himself. This is the only secure basis for freedom.

In pluralist societies, there will always be disagreement about the most appropriate place to begin the quest for human self-knowledge. Some suggest the Torah, others the Koran, and many look to the Christian Gospels. Some insist upon certain philosophical writings, while others look to tradition. Perhaps the best way to begin such a discussion is to find a noncontroversial point upon which all can agree.

The temptation is to identify such a point in terms of man's capacity for thought. This tendency is most explicitly stated in the famous maxim coined by the seventeenth-century metaphysician René Descartes: *cognito ergo sum* (I think, therefore I am). To approach man in this manner is, however, unduly reductionist. It reflects what might be described as a type of "neoangelism," insofar as the person is viewed as a type of pure intelligence—a consciousness—who only possesses a body.

Simple reflection upon our own nature indicates the falsity of this. Humans are not just consciousness. Certainly reason and free will lifts us out of immersion in our organic existence and permits us a degree of self-reflection and a self-directiveness beyond the promptings of our passions. But we are also embodied persons. Our bodies are an essential part of who we are as persons. Our identity is not completely captured in a type of disembodied capacity to think and choose. Indeed, our reason and free will depend on our bodily existence and its ongoing development over time. We are, in effect, thinking organisms, or what some call "embodied intelligent freedom."[39] The most evident manifestation of this is the indisputable fact that human beings *act*.

Human Acts and Human Persons

All human beings act. This is confirmed by our reason, our experience, and all our powers of observation. Human acts are a clear manifestation of each individual's unity of mind and body. When we act, we understand that our body is not a type of instrument at the mind's disposal and direction. Instead, our body takes part in the action, thereby manifesting itself as an inseparable part of our reality as human persons. Human acts prove that we are not disembodied creatures. They prove our essential unity, in all our complexity, as a person.[40]

These may not seem especially radical conclusions. It remains, however, that philosophical anthropology—the study of what man is in order to determine what he should and should not do—has focused almost completely on the study of human consciousness since Descartes' time. This has lead some to imagine that our bodies are somehow separate from our real selves, and may therefore be treated as objects. The consequences for how we view ourselves and others are profound. As Lustiger observes: "Is the body an object, a commodity to be used, or is it an integral part of the human person? And, in the latter case, does it exist outside of the realm of human freedom and, hence, beyond good and evil? That is the fundamental debate."[41]

Reflection on human actions also leads us to recognize that they are more than simply the result of human biology or instinct. Certainly, there are acts, such as the working of our internal organs, which are the product of biology. What does, nonetheless, make human actions different from those of other creatures are two elements which, taken together, make such actions *free*.

One is man's possession of reason, for action needs thought if we are to comprehend the conditions confronting us and we are to triumph over that which is given. An element of rational logic is required if people are to act in a deliberative manner or inquire into what may happen when we act in certain ways. Reason also permits us to act in ways that utilize material things in a creative manner. Such actions may be assessed in terms of technical efficiency and effectiveness.

By itself, however, reason is not enough to make human actions free. Many man-made machines, such as computers, have a type of intelligence built into them. Yet, few would claim that a computer's actions are free. Machines do not possess another specifically human characteristic of human action: that is, free choice. Unless one accepts the reality of free choice, it is impossible to understand *human* action. While an animal can be taught to behave in certain ways, man's capacity for free choice allows him to decide upon and implement an action and then choose a different form of action: to drink a glass of water now, and then go running afterward. A human act thus amounts to what is chosen.

The Rational Will in Action

The question of free choice has perplexed man for centuries. So puzzling and important did Saint Augustine consider the issue that he wrote an entire manuscript on the subject.[42] While there are many senses in which the expression "rational choice" may be used, Finnis provides us with a useful categorization. One is the idea of a fully reasonable choice that, having complied with all the requirements of reason, is good. Then there is the choice that has been shaped by practical reason but also motivated in part by feelings that have partly instrumentalized reason. Lastly, there are decisions that are technically right. Finnis describes these as "identifiable according to some art or technique as the most effective for attaining the relevant technical objective."[43]

How then do reason and free choice mesh together when it comes to human action? And what is the place of what Hobbes and Hume identify as the passions? Perhaps the best analysis of these questions may be found in Aquinas's inquiry into the phenomenon of reason and choice.

According to Aquinas, reason does have an instrumental dimension, but it can also allow man to know greater truths. Reason allows us, for example, to examine political issues and resolve medical problems. Reason also tells us, however, that political matters *should* be explored and that man *may* solve medical questions. This demonstrates that our intelligence can provide us with *reasons for action*, thus taking man toward true wisdom.

This idea is at the root of the vision of free choice outlined by Aquinas: that is, of human intelligence in action. This is a person's will working as an intelligent response to what he comprehends as an opportunity for action.[44] The source of human actions—their motivation—are *reasons;* that is, something intelligible. We act freely when we understand that an action is reasonable and seek to establish a concordance between such reasons and ourselves.

People make free choices when—having judged that they have a reason or reasons to agree to one possible act, and a reason or reasons to adopt alternative but opposing options for action—they choose one option instead of the others.[45] Once the person formally chooses the possibility, it becomes a plan for action. Putting this into effect is what Aquinas calls "command [*imperium*]."[46]

Free choice may therefore be summarized as (1) the contemplation of possibilities that provide reasons for action, followed by (2) the active determination of the value of the object of a possible act, and then (3) the active willing of that act.[47] Such acts cannot therefore be understood as resulting from the inscrutable workings of emotions or biology. It is reason that guides the will, for nothing may be the object of our will unless it is known.

This view of free choice and reason amounts to a vision of the person that contrasts sharply with the anthropology of Thomas Hobbes and David Hume. It suggests that we can make free choices to the extent that we understand and act upon reasons that are not reducible to the emotions; in short, that reason is *not* the slave of the passions.

But, some may ask, does this not risk underestimating the significance of emotions for human decision making, especially in light of the fact that we all experience feelings? Are feelings simply unimportant?

Emotions are important to the moral life, not least because they can often lead us to insights to which reason is initially blind. They can provide us with a legitimate way of choosing between various options, all of which may be reasonable but none of which trumps the other on grounds of reason. The felt strength of an emotion can be a sign of one's commitment to good reasons to act.

Moreover, as Aquinas observed, it is sometimes the case that "good desires work against a perverse reason."[48] Attention to our feelings need not therefore always cause our reason to engage in rationalizations. In some cases, they may even reflect our inner awareness of the wrongness of rationalizing a bad choice.

Feelings must nevertheless be subordinated to reason when it comes to the act of choice. While we can describe the experience of moral good and evil, experience itself cannot define why one action is good and another is wrong. Reason identifies what is desirable, and not vice versa. Only by allowing our rational will to direct our lives, can we become free agents of our decisions.

Acts for Authentic Freedom

There is, however, a deeper significance to free choice that we have not yet considered. This concerns the effects of our actions. We need to recognize that the impacts of our choices go beyond the effect that they may have upon others or the material world.

Aristotle, for one, understood that human action has an inner significance for man. The definitive point of human activity, he held, is the act itself.[49] Freely chosen actions shape not only the external world but also the actor himself, giving moral definition to that person. This difference may be described in terms of the transitive and intransitive dimension of human acts. Aquinas explained this in the following way:

> Action is of two sorts: One sort—action [*actio*] in a strict sense—issues from the agent into something external to change it ... the other sort—properly called activity [*operatio*]—does not issue into something external but remains within the agent itself perfecting it.[50]

Hume, by contrast, flatly denied the intransitive dimension of human action. Philosophers working in the modern tradition rarely speak of it. One searches without success through the works of Mill, Rawls, or Hayek to find it. Even in Mises' monumental study, *Human Action*, it goes unmentioned. All these authors appear to have accepted, consciously or otherwise, Hume's claim that "Actions are by their very nature temporary and perishing; and where they proceed not from some cause in the character and disposition of the person who performed them, they infix not themselves upon him, and can neither redound to his honor, if good, nor infamy, if evil."[51]

Hume provided no reasons for this proposition. Moreover, we know it to be false by virtue of experience and reason.

The transitive effect of an act is what occurs outside us as a result of the action. But the intransitive effect of the same act leaves a mark on us as persons. While this may not be at the forefront of our minds when we make a choice, it is an unavoidable effect of any freely chosen act. This choice lasts within us until we decide to act in a way incompatible with that choice. We thus shape ourselves through our free choices. "Thus," as remarked centuries ago by Saint Gregory of Nyssa, "we are in a certain way our own parents, creating ourselves as we will, by our decisions."[52]

Only from this standpoint can we understand how people develop habits of action—for better or for worse. The more we choose to steal, for example, the more accustomed we become to stealing. To break this habit, we need to choose an action incompatible with stealing. A person may thus choose in his actions to repudiate a past life of crime, while another repudiates his path of virtue by suddenly making unreasonable choices.

An important question arising at this point is whether we are free when we do not act on the basis of reason. One response is to say that acting on the basis of emotions or rationalizations is still to act freely but only insofar as we are acting in what Hayek would call a noncoerced manner. In another sense, however, the answer to this question is surely no. This becomes more evident if we consider the actions of an insane person. Though his actions are not coerced, we do not consider his actions to be freely chosen precisely because the person's rational will is impaired. For centuries, legal systems have permitted defendants to enter the plea of "not-guilty-by-reason-of-insanity." They are, in short, allowed to claim that they were not responsible for their action because their will was not shaped by reason. Defendants making such pleas are maintaining, in effect, to have been a prisoner of "unreason." Unless reason guides the will, there is no free choice, and without free choice, we cannot be regarded as responsible for our actions.

This brings us face-to-face with the profundity of Ratzinger's query: "Is an unreasonable will a free will?" If we believe that humans do not make their choices based on reason, then we can only conclude that our actions are simply the unreasoned, unchosen results of our emotions. Conversely, if we say that our choices are only free if they are directed by reason, then acting freely in the fullest sense means making choices that are reasonable (good), and declining to act in ways that are unreasonable (bad). Freedom thus becomes more than just absence of coercion. It is, rather, the fruit of rational choices.

Reasons for Action

The coherence of the understanding of freedom articulated here depends very much upon what we understand to be a reason for action, or what some philosophers call a "basic good."[53] As observed by the liberal jurist, Joseph Raz, the fact that someone desires to do something is not a reason for performing a particular action.[54] Reasonable persons will hold their beliefs not because it feels right or it "just happens" to be something they have chosen but because their reason tells them that it is true. As Raz explains:

People have goals and have desires for reasons. They believe that the objects of their desires or their pursuits are valuable.... This reason-dependent character of goals and desires entails that any person who has a goal or a desire believes, if he has a minimal understanding of their nature, that if he came to believe that there were no reasons to pursue the goal or the desire, he would no longer have them.[55]

But how do we come to know genuine reasons for truly human action? Put another way, what are the reasons for action—the *basic* goods—that reflect the essence of what it is to be a human person?

In Aristotle, we find a way of identifying the basic goods at the core of our identity as free persons. Aristotle suggested that by determining the objects of our distinctly human acts, we identify our truly *human* potentialities and, thus, the essence of what it is to be human.

We are looking therefore for fundamental reasons for action that humans undertake for their own sake, that require no other reference to another object or purpose because our reason tells us that they are in themselves good for man[56]— that they are basic, intelligible goods, intrinsic elements that inform us of *what we are* as human persons, and what we are capable of becoming if we want to be truly human.

There are, of course, many intelligible goods that are instrumental but not basic. People exercise, for example, to reduce excessive weight. Losing excessive weight is a good reason for acting, but it is only intelligibly good because it contributes to being healthy and staying alive.[57] The free choice to exercise presupposes that human life is a basic good to be promoted and protected.[58] Life is therefore an ultimate reason for a choice. So, too, is friendship. The end of true friendship is its very continuity. It is expressed in the acts of two people for the sake of each other. These express the essence of friendship. In itself, then, friendship is not a means to an end; indeed, friendship has no independent existence beyond the choice of two people to be friends.

Another example of a basic good—a reason for action that needs no further explanation—might be "religion." This may be illustrated by imagining a person leaving his house on a Saturday. Why, we ask, is he doing so? If the answer is "He is going to synagogue," we may inquire, "Why is he attending synagogue?" If the response is "Because he is a religious Jew," we may further inquire, "Why does he choose to be a practicing Jew?" At this point, one could mention factors such as his upbringing or his desire to see close friends. But one answer to the question of why the man chooses to go to synagogue, that requires no further explanation, is that Judaism *is* the man's religion. It results from his choice to reflect reasonably upon the question of whether or not there is an ultimate transcendent source of good that provides a compelling explanation of life. Going to synagogue reflects his choice to order his life on the basis of the conclusions of his inquiry. Though the man may not consciously think of this reason for action each time he goes to synagogue, it remains at the root of his choice to do so.

None of us begin to choose freely until we begin to comprehend intelligible, basic goods. The acts of a child conform to patterns established by his instinct and experience. As he grows, his actions begin to reflect the emergence of his rational will. Soon he is using his reason to solve problems in an imaginative rather than in an unconscious way. He also starts comprehending that there are many reasons to act, and that they cannot all be chosen in the one action. Thus, not only is there opportunity to decide but a requirement to make choices.

Instances of basic reasons for action have been identified by a range of scholars. They include (1) *life* and the component aspects of its fullness such as health; (2) *friendship* or harmony between persons; (3) *marriage*; (4) *knowledge* of truth; (5) *aesthetic experience*; (6) *skillful performance* in work or play; (7) *religion* (as explained above); and (8) *practical reasonableness*—the shaping of our participation in other basic goods by our determination of our particular commitments, our selecting of specific projects, and our acts in pursuing these objectives.[59]

When we act in ways that allow us to participate in a basic good, we actualize the potential that is ours by virtue of being human; that is, we *fulfill* ourselves in the way that humans ought to. Conversely, when we act in ways that contradict such goods (such as intentionally working in a less-than-skillful way), we damage ourselves inasmuch as we intentionally perpetuate an absence of something about us as humans that ought to be.

This does not mean that acting in authentically human ways obliges us to try to participate in every one of these goods in any one of our freely chosen actions. This is impossible. We cannot simultaneously study (the good of knowledge) while running a marathon (the good of skillful performance). On the one hand, our choice of one good over another inevitably means that we do not participate in other goods through that particular choice. This is an unintended side-effect: We foresee that it will result from our action, but we do not choose it.

On the other hand, we can choose ends that directly violate other basic goods. The Waffen SS soldier who fights for Hitler may do so skillfully. In doing so, however, the soldier violates the good of practical reasonableness by using his military skills to defend a genocidal regime. Upon his transfer to Auschwitz, the same soldier may prove adept at operating the gas chambers. His skillful performance, however, directly contributes to the intentional destruction of innocent life, thereby rendering his action unreasonable.

This is why the good of practical reasonableness is particularly important. It helps us to avoid directly violating the basic goods. It also enables us to cope with the fact that all of us have far more reasonable wishes that we could ever hope to satisfy in a lifetime. Moreover, different people have diverse possibilities of integral fulfillment. Each person has, for example, special abilities. These make certain choices more practicably reasonable for that individual and less so for others. While a person may have great talents as a scholar, his abilities as a mountain climber may be nonexistent. Being practically reasonable, he should choose to focus on his scholarly talents, and leave mountain climbing as a career choice for others. No good is violated in this commitment. By contrast, an unreasonable action would be for the same person to place his scholarly skills at the service of a criminal regime.

Our full adherence to prohibitions against acting contrary to the basic goods is thus harmonious with the view that there are many right, albeit incompatible, ways of acting reasonably. The basic goods give rise to a potentially infinite number of ways for people to fulfill themselves. The very existence of these incommensurable basic goods—incommensurable, as none can be reduced to any of the others—thus is what makes apparent the truth that we really can freely choose.

Of course, some people's ability to choose particular ends may be limited by, for instance, their economic circumstances. It nevertheless remains that no one can force them to perform actions that lead to a loss of self-mastery and a diminution of their flourishing precisely as human beings, for while there are numerous ways of intentionally acting against a basic good, we can always decline to do so: We can *always* choose *not* to destroy life, *not* to embrace ignorance, *not* to work badly, *not* to behave foolishly—even in the most horrendous of circumstances and perhaps at the price of losing one's own life. The writer of some of the most epic novels of the twentieth century, Aleksandr Solzhenitsyn, understood this when he proclaimed in his 1970 Nobel Prize lecture:

> There is one simple step a simple courageous man can take—not to take part in the lie, not to give his support to false actions. Let this principle [i.e., the lie that masks the evil] enter the world and even dominate the world—but not through me.[60]

Nor should we underestimate the potential for people to choose the basic goods, even in conditions of extreme hardship. The Holocaust survivor and psychologist, Viktor Frankl, sees this as the most vivid evidence of the reality of free choice:

> We who lived in concentration camps can remember the men who walked through the huts comforting others, giving away their last piece of bread. They may have been few in number, but they offer sufficient proof that everything can be taken away from a man but one thing: the last of the human freedoms—to choose one's attitude in any given set of circumstances, to choose one's own way.[61]

Liberty as Self-Government

The understanding of freedom articulated in this chapter, especially its reliance upon the idea of basic reasons for action, is certainly controversial. Objections abound but so, too, do responses. Some have questioned whether, for example, knowledge, life, or practical reasonableness are universally recognized across cultures as essential human goods. Powerful evidence, however, attests to man's recognition of the basic goods regardless of time, place, and culture.[62] The same point may be put negatively: There has never been a culture in which it is regarded as reasonable and good to be a coward, or to be proud of lying.

As illustrated, the Aristotelian method of asking questions about the aims of specifically human acts provides philosophical evidence that basic goods exist. However, having identified such goods, we are also able to identify those actions that do not contribute to the fulfillment of our humanness. If, for example, knowledge ought to be treated as a form of excellence, it is unreasonable for anyone to deny that error and ignorance are evils that no persons can reasonably wish for themselves or others.[63] Nor is there any reason to be neutral between death and life, or skillful performance and incompetence. If this is true, then we can confidently state that those who treat knowledge, beauty, or any other basic good as irrelevant, are being irrational.

This understanding of reason and free choice has particular implications for what we understand a truly free society to be. A society informed by a vision of man as a knowing, freely choosing, embodied creature, will be very different to one in which man is understood as an essentially emotion-driven creature whose reason is purely instrumental. Once we take the totality of man into account, we recognize that there is more to a free society than just minimization of coercion. Freedom itself requires that we act in a fully reasonable manner and avoid rationalizations.

The same view of man and human freedom also allows us to speak of liberty in a way that transcends Berlin's alternatives of negative and positive liberty. This is *liberty as self-government*. This understands freedom as something to be won. Liberty as self-government—integral liberty—links the subjective dimension of human existence, manifest in the reality of free choice, with the objective dimension that reflects man's unique capacity to know that there are basic goods that transcend time, feelings, and preference in their truthfulness.

We must, however, consider the consequences of integral liberty for the fact of disagreement that continues to characterize modern society. At first sight, to speak of a society characterized by a commitment to integral liberty appears futile, primarily because the prospects of securing universal recognition of basic goods seems utopian.

Yet liberty as self-government need not be understood as at odds with societies that value choice and difference. Integral liberty takes free choice seriously. Moreover, there are ways of coping with the fact of disagreement without denying the truthfulness of the basic goods, for if skepticism is wrong, and that all can indeed know the basic reasons for actions, there is no reason why public discussion of controversial questions should focus only on how we control the disagreement. We should have some expectation that we can surmount the misconceptions at the heart of the discord.

Being a free person does, however, involve making choices, and the people and the choices are many. Hence, even if everyone only makes choices based on reasons for action and thus free of rationalization, many choices would still be incompatible. The reality that everyone sometimes makes unreasonable choices further complicates matters.

We are thus inevitably drawn toward studying how order may prevail in a society of freely choosing and reasoning persons. Here, law has a role to play in coordinating the millions of choices made by individuals and groups every day. While the manner in which people learn to become free does not occur primarily through observance of rules, law does play a subsidiary role in this formation. It is therefore appropriate that we assess the function of law in shaping a free society, especially what we will call its *moral ecology*, for if the value of liberty depends upon its being used well, we should not presume that legal protection should immediately be given to empty or unreasonable choices.

Notes

1. Livy, *Livy* (London: Heinemann, 1919–1959), vol. 10, bk. 34, 49.

2. Charles de Montesquieu, *The Spirit of the Laws*, ed. A. Cohler, (Cambridge: Cambridge University Press, 1989), c. 12, 1, 2.

3. See G. W. F. Hegel, *Philosophy of Right*, trans. T. M. Knox (Oxford: Oxford University Press, 1942), 215.

4. See Isaiah Berlin, "Two Concepts of Liberty," in *The Proper Study of Mankind: An Anthology of Essays* (New York: Farrar, Straus and Giroux, 1997), 194–203.

5. Berlin, "Two Concepts of Liberty," 205.

6. Richard Rorty, "Taking Philosophy Seriously," *New Republic*, 11 April 1988, 33.

7. See Richard Rorty, "The Seer of Prague," *New Republic*, 1 July 1991, 31.

8. Hayek, *Constitution*, 11.

9. Ibid., 13.

10. Ibid., 15.

11. Ibid., 16.

12. *Planned Parenthood of Southeastern PA. v. Casey*, 505 U.S. 833, 951 (1992) (O'Connor, Kennedy and Souter, JJ, joint opinion).

13. See Thomas More, *The Complete Works of Saint Thomas More*, vol. 13, *A Treatise Upon the Passion*, ed. Garry E. Haupt (New Haven, Conn.: Yale University Press, 1976), 226/14.

14. Thomas More, *The English Works of Sir Thomas More*, ed. W. E. Campbell et al., vol. 1 (London: Eyre & Spottiswoode, 1931), 495.

15. See Hayek, *Constitution*, 133.

16. Ibid., 29.

17. Ibid., 31.

18. Ibid., 41.

19. Ibid.

20. Ibid., 42.

21. See Germain Grisez and Russell Shaw, *Beyond the New Morality: The Responsibilities of Freedom*, 3d ed., (Notre Dame, Ind.: University of Notre Dame Press, 1988), 36.

22. Hayek, *Constitution*, 63: citing Hume, *Treatise*, bk. 3, pt. 1, sec. 1.

23. See Hayek, *Constitution*, 63.

24. Ibid., 436, fn. 37.

25. Ibid., 406.

26. See Aristotle, *Ethics*, V.

27. Joseph Ratzinger, "Truth and Freedom," *Communio: International Catholic Review*, 23, no. 1 (1996): 17 (emphasis added).

28. See John Finnis, *Fundamentals of Ethics* (Washington, D.C.: Georgetown University Press, 1983), 7.

29. See Tocqueville, *Democracy*, 444, 464, 548.

30. Hobbes, *Leviathan*, pt. 1, chap. 8.

31. Joseph Ratzinger, "Preserve Your Christian Roots," *Inside the Vatican*, 10, no. 2 (March 2002): 74.

32. John Finnis, *Aquinas: Moral, Political, and Legal Theory* (Oxford: Oxford University Press, 1998), 60.

33. See Joseph de Maistre, *Considerations on France* (Cambridge: Cambridge University Press, 1994), 76.

34. See Thomas Aquinas, *Summa Theologiae*, ed. T. Gilby, O.P. (London: Blackfriars, 1963), I-II, 100, 1c.

35. Karl Marx and Friedrich Engels, *Works*, vol. 3 (London: Penguin, 1971), 33.

36. Ratzinger, "Truth and Freedom," 17.

37. See John Stuart Mill, *A System of Logic* (London: Longmans, 1859), bk. 6, chaps. 2 and 11.

38. Jean-Marie Lustiger, *Choosing God—Chosen by God* (San Francisco: Ignatius Press, 1991), 181.

39. See Benedict M. Ashley and Kevin D. O'Rourke, *Health Care Ethics: A Theological Analysis*, 4th ed. (Washington, D.C.: Georgetown University, 1996), 6.

40. See Luke Gormally, *Euthanasia, Clinical Practice and the Law* (London: Linarce Centre, 1994), 111–66.

41. Lustiger, *Choosing God*, 255.

42. See Augustine of Hippo, *Contra academicos: de beata vita; de ordine; de magistro; de libero arbitrio* (Turnhout: Brepols, 1970).

43. John Finnis, "Natural Law and Legal Reasoning," in *Natural Law Theory: Contemporary Essays*, ed. Robert P. George (Oxford: Clarendon Press, 1992), 141.

44. "For one's will is in one's intelligence . . . the source of this sort of appetite is understanding, that is, the intellectual act that is somehow moved by something intelligible." Thomas Aquinas, *Sententia Super Metaphysican*, XII, 7, ed. Robert Busa, in *Thomae Aquinatis Opera Omnia cum Hypertextibus in CD-ROM*, rev. ed. (Milan: Editoria Elettronica Editel, 1996).

45. See Finnis, *Aquinas*, 63–78.

46. Aquinas, *ST*, I-II, q. 17, a. 1.

47. For a more detailed differentiation, see Finnis, *Aquinas*, 71.

48. Aquinas, *ST*, II-II, q. 155, a. 1, ad. 2.

49. See Aristotle, *Nicomachean Ethics* (Oxford: Oxford University Press, 1998), 6, 4: 1140b3–6.

50. Thomas Aquinas, *Quaestiones Disputatae de Veritate*, q. 8, a. 6c.

51. Hume, *A Treatise of Human Nature*, bk. 2, pt. 2, sec. 2.

52. Saint Gregory of Nyssa, *De Vita Moysis*, trans. A. J. Malherbe and E. Ferguson (New York: Paulist Press, 1978), II, 2–3.

53. This section follows closely the respective accounts of Grisez and Finnis in *Beyond the New Morality*, chap. 7 and *Natural Law*, 60–99.

54. See Raz, *The Morality of Freedom*, 89.

55. Ibid., 140.

56. Aquinas explained the self-evident nature of these reasons for action in the following manner: "something which is desirable to sensory appetite [*concupiscibile*] but is not an intelligible good [*intelligibile bonum*] is an apparent good. A primary good must be willable, that is, desirable by intellectual appetite (for will is in understanding, and not merely in the appetite of sensory desire). . . . But what is desired by intellectual appetite is desired because it seems good in itself." Aquinas, Meta. XII, 7 n. 4.

57. See Grisez and Shaw, *Beyond the New Morality*, 79–84.

58. One can also regard a basic good in some instances as instrumental to another basic good. A person may want to stay alive (a basic good) so as to care for friends and meet other commitments.

59. To act in a practically reasonable manner, Finnis states, means always following the following basic principles: (1) Have a coherent plan of life; (2) Show no arbitrary preference among goods or persons; (4) Maintain sufficient detachment from, but also commitment to, your projects; (5) Be efficient (within reason) in your actions; (6) Show respect for every basic good in every act; (7) Respect the common good's requirements; and (8) Follow one's conscience. See Finnis, *Natural Law*, chap. 5.

60. Alexander Solzhenitsyn, *Nobel Prize Lecture*, sec. 7, trans. Bethell (London: Stenvalley Press, 1973), 53.

61. Viktor Frankl, *Man's Search for Meaning*, rev. ed., trans. Ilse Lasch (New York: Simon and Schuster, 1962), 65.

62. See, for example, Aquinas, *ST*, I-II, q. 94, a. 2. Cf. Morris Ginsberg, *On the Diversity of Morals* (London: Royal Anthropological Institute of Great Britain and Ireland, 1956); Alexander MacBeath, *Experiments in Living: A Study of the Nature and Foundations of Ethics or Morals in the Light of Recent Work in Social Anthropology* (London: Macmillan, 1952); Richard A. Beis, "Some Contributions of Anthropology to Ethics," *Thomist*, 28 (1964): 174.

63. See Finnis, *Natural Law*, 106.

4

Law and Liberty

Law in general is human reason insofar as it governs all the peoples of the earth.

—Charles de Montesquieu[1]

The question of how a society of free persons is ordered has always been central to philosophical, legal, and political debate. A predictable controversy is the extent to which law can—or should—contribute to the formation of a free society characterized by commitment to certain goods. An associated debate concerns the use of legal coercion to deter people from choosing other ends. The number of people who disagree, for example, that pornography demeans the dignity of those posing is relatively small. More contentious is whether the law ought to forbid people from purchasing this literature. Some regard such laws as inherently unjust because they are perceived to constitute illegitimate intrusion upon human autonomy. Surely the conservative philosopher Roger Scruton does not exaggerate when he claims that many have come to imagine that a question of individual liberty is somehow at issue with every question of law.[2]

Of course, it is not true that every legal argument or issue of justice is reducible to questions of liberty. Nevertheless, contemporary disputes over subjects ranging from free speech and the use of narcotics, to abortion, cloning, and euthanasia do reflect profound disagreement over the relationship between law and human liberty. It is not our intention to examine any of these particular issues in this chapter. Instead, we consider some of the deeper matters at stake, precisely

51

because of their powerful implications for defining the nature of a truly free social order. It is a simple exercise to demonstrate how law can suppress human freedom. The English jurist H. L. A. Hart reminds us, however, that a legal order can highly respect liberty and still be deeply iniquitous in its implications for other dimensions of human existence.[3] The difficult task of law is to support our reason against the impulses of our passions—to guide a reasoning people capable of self-governance but also of self-abasement, without unduly undermining our scope for free choice.

The Order of Rules

Even cursory attention to the writings of most self-described liberal scholars soon indicates that, far from being libertines or anarchists, they invariably emphasize that social order requires binding rules. For all his contempt for absolutism, a nineteenth-century French liberal like François Guizot could remark, "It is not true that man is absolute master of himself, that his will is his legitimate sovereign, that at no moment, under no circumstances does anyone have right over him without his consent."[4] Or, as he stated elsewhere: "considered in isolation and in himself, the individual does not therefore dispose of himself arbitrarily and according to his will alone. His will is not his legitimate sovereign."[5]

Many liberals such as Rawls and Hayek regard law as a key institution—perhaps *the* key institution—of civilization. In *The Constitution of Liberty*, Hayek goes so far as to describe law as "the science of liberty."[6] Part of law's uniqueness, Hayek maintained, is that it was not invented by anyone. Rather, law emerged through a type of natural selection process, whereby unconscious habits developed into explicit, more abstract rules that embody particular information that we take into account before acting. In this way, law permits each person's legitimate autonomy to be identified in advance, while simultaneously allowing individuals to act freely within this defined sphere.[7]

In several senses, Hayek's analysis rings true. To pursue freedom is, it seems, to define the restrictions that are its prerequisite. Sets of defined, publicly acknowledged, and consistently applied coercive rules can create spheres of personal freedom within which one can act without being arbitrarily subjected to another's will. A just system of civil law, for example, provides people with a public facility for regulating their private interactions via the law of torts, contracts, and property. Hayek's understanding of law also appears to have absorbed something of Edmund Burke's stress upon the accumulated wisdom of centuries built into many laws—a wisdom we often do not realize has been lost until a law is abolished.

There are, nonetheless, difficulties with Hayek's understanding of how law protects human liberty. While laws do evolve within certain traditions, this need not imply that they cannot be explained in terms of reason.[8] A more significant problem, however, is the manner in which Hayek's position distances law from the demands of the good and, therefore, integral liberty.

Bentham, Hobbes, and Hume are among those who, like Hayek, regard law as primarily concerned with rules rather than with the good.[9] Hume maintained, for example, that law did not proceed from an innate sense of what is just.[10] Law was essentially a matter of morally neutral social fact rather than any truth about the demands of justice. At most, Hayek is willing to associate law with "thin theories of the good." An example of such a theory would be the principle that law should protect pluralism, whatever the content of that pluralism. Law, from this standpoint, concerns the rules under which people make choices; it should not express what reason suggests that people should and should not choose.

Such arguments are ultimately self-refuting. To suggest, even by implication, that law *ought* not to be concerned with what constitutes human fulfillment—presumably because this would unjustly violate the autonomy of those skeptical about such matters—is to breach one's own claims to neutrality about the good (not least by utilizing the language of obligation). It is also to go beyond a thin theory of the good by implying that there is some *deeper value* to autonomy that outweighs all other possible goods.

Moral Ecology and Legal Paternalism

By definition, the only jurisprudential alternative to thin theories of the good are those based upon visions of what it means to live a good and fulfilling life. The beginnings of this view of law may be found in recognition that every person begins his life as a tabula rasa. We consequently have to grow to understand what is good and reasonable, and, therefore, at the core of human freedom.

Yet, even if we accept the idea of integral liberty as true, we are immediately confronted by the fact that a range of external obstacles impede the achievement of such self-mastery. Aquinas observed centuries ago that immoral practices and customs would tend to dominate in a given society.[11] He specified that many of the mistakes and rationalizations that occur in a community over long periods of time will become concretely embodied in particular customs and practices. Aquinas also recognized that some will always find it difficult to understand why certain actions are unreasonable and therefore a path away from freedom, for such understanding can involve complex arguments, many of which presume much background knowledge.

Aquinas's consciousness of these problems led him to insist that law *ought* to play a role in directing us to integral fulfillment. He did not think that "man could suffice for himself in the matter of this training, since the perfection of virtue consists chiefly in withdrawing man from undue pleasures."[12] Aristotle similarly stated that it was "difficult to get from youth up a right training for virtue if one has not been brought up under right laws."[13] The insight shared by Aristotle and Aquinas was that while people's actions shape the external environment—ideas, narratives, institutions, prevailing opinions and practices, sources of shame and acclaim—the same framework that constitutes a society's moral culture can facilitate or impede people's reasonable choices.

The word "culture" embraces everything through which people develop their many bodily, moral, intellectual, and spiritual qualities. The formation of culture requires human creativity and intelligence and is expressed through human action. Plants and animals live and act but have no culture. Culture is something distinctly human, since man's actions are uniquely creative of it. Being its source, man need not become the prisoner of any one culture.

Human culture may be expressed and objectified in various products, practices, and institutions that in turn influence their human creators. These manifestations include material objects but also the different ways of living arising from the diverse manner of using things, expressing oneself, forming customs, establishing laws, and cultivating the mind. Culture thus also embraces all concepts and perceptions existent within a given society, especially those to which the society's members ascribe higher value.

Cultures may, however, also embody failures to recognize that particular practices are, in fact, unreasonable. An example might be the custom of human sacrifice that prevailed in the pre-Conquest societies of Central and South America societies. To the extent that the moral ecologies of these societies embraced this practice and systematically violated the good of life, they were corrupt.

While humans possess the capacity for free choice, we are not isolated from all the actions, customs, and institutions that surround us. Even the private acts of individuals can and do have public consequences. A child, for example, who sees his father reading pornography may develop an unhealthy view of women and consequently find it harder to resist interacting both privately and publicly with women in ways that demean their dignity as persons. By the same token, if our choices are influenced by a moral ecology grounded in a vision of man as one who can know basic reasons for action, our choices are likely to reflect very different priorities.

Law is in part an expression and a shaper of human culture. It thus influences the choices we make. If the law treats, for example, the good of marriage as just another contractual arrangement, it becomes harder for those who recognize marriage as a basic good to act in ways that reflect the truth about marriage.

Of course, law is not sufficient for fostering a moral culture that encourages people's development of integral liberty. Tocqueville, for one, was careful to remind us that "Laws are always unsteady when unsupported by mores; mores are the only tough and durable power in a nation."[14] At the same time, we should not underestimate law's potential to mold a community's moral ecology. Legal prohibitions can, for example, discourage us from making choices that contribute to our inner disintegration. They can also deflect us from being bad examples to others.

This is not to suggest that law should have the primary role in shaping the moral culture. It is merely to state that law has *a* role and, at a minimum, should not directly promote any activity that damages this moral ecology. Rather, it should prudently do what it can to protect a society's moral ecology against the harmful acts of individuals and groups, especially when appeals to their practical reasonableness fail.

In this sense, we can begin to speak about law as embracing a type of "harm-principle" that goes beyond that defined by Mill:

> The sole end for which mankind is warranted, individually or collectively, in interfering with the liberty of action of any of their number, is self-protection. That the only purpose for which power can be rightfully exercised over any member of a civilized community, against his will, is to prevent harm to others. His own good, either physical or moral, is not sufficient warrant.[15]

Though Mill's words have been subject to competing explanations, his "great simple principle" essentially holds that those vices of conduct and inclination that have no significant relationship to peace and justice are not the concern of law.

Insofar as this principle reflects the need to respect the necessary element of self-determination involved in any genuinely free choice, it is consistent with the promotion of integral liberty. Once, however, we acknowledge the potential of a society's moral ecology to hinder significantly people's ability to achieve integral liberty, we begin to understand that various "private" vices can have a negative impact upon justice insofar as they detract from everyone's entitlement to live in an environment which helps (without attempting to guarantee) all to achieve integral fulfillment. Once such harm is inflicted upon an aspect of this environment, it becomes in principle a legitimate concern of the law.

A Violation of Freedom?

This understanding of law's appropriate relationship to liberty contradicts most contemporary liberal jurisprudence. A prominent expression of such thought may be found in John Rawls' 1996 book *Political Liberalism*. Law, according to Rawls, should avoid passing judgment upon certain practices. "Which moral judgments are true," Rawls states, "is not a matter for political liberalism."[16] Hence, law ought not to constrain human autonomy on the grounds that a particular concept of what constitutes human fulfillment is more truthful than another.[17]

As an alternative to truth-based theories, Rawls presents an idea of liberty and law that he deems valid because of its potential to establish an "overlapping consensus" in pluralist societies. This consensus, he holds, should be based on a degree of accord about just conditions for collaboration among reasonable individuals in democratic societies. Instead of attempting to determine which of the competing religious and secularist doctrines is true, Rawls claims that democratic societies ought to focus on establishing "a liberal political concept that . . . nonliberal doctrines might be able to endorse."[18] According to Rawls, these conditions will be just inasmuch as the people offering them reasonably believe that they have a reasonable chance of acceptance by other citizens according to their "common human reason."[19]

Such a "criterion of reciprocity," as Rawls describes it, excludes people from presenting arguments about just conditions upon the basis that they are true. This, he believes, violates the fact of reasonable pluralism. Significantly, Rawls does not claim that his own view is valid or true. He thus joins those who have abandoned the idea that basic philosophical truths can be known by the human mind, and that such truths can consequently serve as the foundation for authentically human societies. Rawls does not, however, base his position on an explicit adherence to skepticism. Rather, Rawls maintains that to claim that his own position is true would be to violate the necessary conditions for freedom and justice in pluralist societies. Truth, in his view, should be supplanted as the measure for correct law by an idea of the reasonable. The good and the true, from Rawls' viewpoint, are different from the reasonable and the right.

With more than a hint of irony, John Finnis points out that this leads to the odd conclusion that "many concepts of public policy are 'reasonable' although quite untrue."[20] It is not, however, obvious that reason obliges us to discard our desire for truth or to stay silent about truth. Reasonable people may indeed take different positions on a range of questions. This hardly suggests, however, that all views are equally reasonable.[21]

In any event, Rawls' position is not as devoid of truth-claims as he supposes. His political liberalism assumes that there is something *wrong* with viewing law as one means of fostering an environment that helps people to choose basic goods. It does so because any such law would apparently constitute unreasonable violation of some people's autonomy: That is, those who do not recognize human flourishing as the reasonable end of human choice, or those who want to choose ends that lead to inner disintegration. Autonomy, then, is Rawls' trump card: It is the unspoken *good* that almost always overrides other considerations. Needless to say, this is not a neutral position. Rawls' violation of his own principles only underlines the validity of an observation by another liberal, William Galston, that "every contemporary liberal theory that begins by promising to do without a substantive theory of the good ends by betraying that promise."[22]

Another liberal alternative to the view of law and liberty that we have associated with Aristotle and Aquinas has been articulated by the philosopher Ronald Dworkin, most notably in his 1977 book *Taking Rights Seriously.*[23] Unlike Rawls, Dworkin does not disdain truth-claims. Instead, Dworkin proposes that law should be based on the truth of a particular principle: that the law should treat all people with equal respect and concern.[24] Law violates this right to equality, Dworkin claims, whenever it impedes individual liberty on the grounds that one person's concept of human fulfillment is superior to another's.[25] It follows that laws ought to operate in ways that do not rely upon acceptance of any particular concept of the good life.

A prominent difficulty with Dworkin's vision is that at no point does he explain from where he derives this right to equality. There is also something unsound, Robert P. George remarks, with Dworkin's assumption that a legal concern for the good of persons necessarily indicates a type of disrespect for those individuals whose preferred behavior is legally restricted.[26] In fact, such legal limitations may, as Finnis points out, actually

> manifest, not contempt, but a sense of the equal worth and human dignity of those people, whose conduct is outlawed precisely on the ground that it expresses a serious misconception of, and actually degrades, human worth and dignity, and this degrades their own personal worth and dignity, along with that of others who may be induced to share in or emulate their degradation.[27]

In response to these and similar criticisms, Dworkin has restated his position. He does not deny that certain private habits (such as reading pornography) do damage a society's moral environment.[28] He even accepts that a "right to vice" cannot be derived from a "general right to autonomy." Nonetheless, equality of concern and respect (still undefined in terms of origin), he insists, is violated whenever the law imposes constraints upon people because of a theory with which they cannot agree without undermining their own sense of self-worth. In Dworkin's words, "no self-respecting person who believes that a particular way to live is most valuable to him can accept that this way of life is base or degrading."[29]

This argument is equally unsatisfactory. In the first instance, Dworkin unreasonably rules out the possibility that people may recognize that their past choices were wrong. This development in no way undermines their self-respect. If anything, acknowledgment of error is liberating insofar as it underscores our ability to know and live in truth. Some people may even retrospectively appreciate that the law inhibited them from acting on their wrong choices. Secondly, as Robert P. George remarks, the experience of running afoul of the criminal code may actually assist some persons to realize that their choice or pattern of behavior was unworthy of them. Any resulting diminution of self-respect would follow from the offenders' *self*-realization of the unworthiness of their choice. To this extent, the existence of the legal prohibition would simply affirm that those who formulated the law share the offenders' recognition of the shamefulness of certain actions.[30] Lastly, the fact that the law prohibits an action does not necessarily mean that anyone is being forced to accept an argument about the good. In democracies, for example, people remain free to disagree publicly with any law, and even to try to repeal particular laws.

One might go further and ask a question that strikes at the very root of Dworkin's argument: Are all opinions and views actually entitled to equal respect, as Dworkin appears to insist, even though we may not approve of the action proceeding from such claims? In response, we may ask: What possible reason could there be for "respecting" Stalin's view that show-trials and State terrorism are expedient, or the Nazi position that the Jewish people ought to be exterminated? The mere fact that people have freely arrived at such conclusions is hardly sufficient for these opinions to be respected.

Though Dworkin's approach to the relationship between law and liberty differs from that of Rawls, both scholars are concerned with attempting to resolve the same important problem: How *do* free societies cope with the fact of pluralism? Rawls and Dworkin believe that justice in such societies requires laws to be based on what can be presently agreed upon by all members of society, whatever their disagreements about other subjects. The question of whether such agreements are rationally coherent (in the sense of accordance with truth) is consequently irrelevant. The logic underlying Rawls' and Dworkin's respective positions suggests that law ought to define rules that allow as many individuals as possible in a given society to pursue very different visions of happiness, based on varying ideas about freedom, and diverse concepts of the meaning of life. Law must consequently stand above competing views of the good and not intervene in those questions about which a society is deeply divided.

In making such claims, these liberal theories infringe their own primary rules. To claim that we *ought* not impose rules based on controversial truth claims upon others is to propose a view of the right and the good. This liberal view of law thus violates its own emphasis upon avoiding truth claims. It also amounts to imposing a philosophy of law upon those who believe that law should be based on truth-claims that can be sustained by reason. There is thus a self-refuting rationale contained within the liberal position that law ought not to privilege a particular view of what people may choose, inasmuch as this amounts to according legal privileges to the liberal view of the role of law vis-à-vis human choice.

Protecting Autonomy

Though the liberal theories assessed thus far are unable to provide coherent explanations concerning why the law ought to protect human autonomy, there remains one very serious reason for the law to try to do so. The genuine importance of autonomy becomes evident once we recognize that it is a necessary prerequisite for integral liberty. No one can be forced to choose self-evident reasons for actions. A "coerced free choice" is a contradiction in terms. Achieving integral liberty requires us to exercise our rational will correctly. Moreover, the opportunity of choices that lead to integral liberty assumes the prospect of decisions that do not.

The fact, however, that people need to make free choices does not mean that law has no role in this area. As noted, there are some good reasons why law should place some restrictions on our ability to do as we please. The issue is, thus, how law can protect legitimate autonomy without embracing the unreasonable claims associated with Rawls and Dworkin or, conversely, succumbing to authoritarian temptations.

Law as Coordinator

The beginning of an answer to this question lies in identifying the nature of the community that law is meant to serve. Law is an instrument of that community we call "the State" or "the political community." By "the State," we do not have in mind "the government." We are referring to the community served by a government.

From the standpoint of integral liberty, there are two types of community.[31] First, there are those communities, such as the family and Churches, whose very formation actualizes a basic reason for action. A community of religious believers, for example, acts together in ways that express its conclusions concerning the truth about the ultimate origin and meaning of human existence. In that sense, this community directly participates in the good of religion, a good commonly pursued (at least ostensibly!) by all of its members.

The second type of community is the association that serves to realize instrumental goods. It seeks to establish those conditions that facilitate but do not directly realize people's actualization of basic goods. The political community falls into this category.

By themselves, neither the political community nor its law can directly instantiate a good like friendship or work. Law can assist, however, in securing the conditions that help people to participate in basic goods. These conditions are the *common* good of all members of the political community. The law helps to establish such conditions, not least by dealing with particular ineradicable problems of a human society.

One such difficulty is the fact that millions of choices are made every day in a society. Some choices are compatible with each other. Others are not. Indeed even a political community composed of completely virtuous people would require an authority to coordinate their rational choices for different goods. In the modern world, for example, people often need to travel long distances in order to participate in particular goods, such as the skillful performance of work. Thus, we have traffic laws. While reason itself will not tell us that requiring all people to drive on the left is better than on the right, it does tell us that a decision needs to made by someone concerning which side of the road people should drive on. In this instance, the creation of such laws provides grounds for viewing actions that are otherwise reasonable (driving to a destination) as unreasonable (driving on a particular side of the road to that destination).

What should, however, be noted is that this coordinating function of law does not assume that law should be neutral. It is directed to assisting people to realize integral liberty. Certainly law does involve an ingredient of technical analysis insofar as it seeks to settle conflict through reflection upon rules that designate which actions are legally acceptable. Nonetheless, these rules do, at least indirectly, seek to enhance everyone's ability to achieve fulfillment. They also enhance human autonomy by helping to establish conditions that make integral liberty a real possibility, not least by preventing the emergence of anarchic situations that make it harder for people to exercise their autonomy.

Law as Educator

An objection that may be raised at this point is that classical legal theory has always insisted that the requirements of law apply only to forms of stipulated conduct and that law should not directly concern itself with the motives that people have for conforming to that law.[32] In itself this claim is true. Yet, the same classical theory also maintains that law is concerned with the practical matter of how humans act and what we ought to do. This is reflected in the language shared by law and morality. Even the twentieth-century's most prominent positivist jurist, Hans Kelsen, conceded that "by [legal] 'norm' we mean something ought to be or ought to happen, especially that a human being ought to act in a specific way."[33] Law uses terms such as "right," "responsibility," "ought," and "obligation" when reflecting upon a variety of possible circumstances in which people may act. It also forbids people from certain actions and uses language such as "ought not" and invokes sanctions to this effect. The language of morality does the same. It speaks of "oughts" and, in some cases, refers to specific sanctions as applicable to certain actions. To this extent, both law and moral reasoning ask us to think about what it is right or wrong, reasonable or unreasonable, for us to choose.

What, then, is the significance of this view of law for autonomy? The answer is that law has a pedagogical function. It helps to provide information about matters (such as the truth of the basic goods) that people need before making reasonable choices while simultaneously providing important room for free choice.

This may be illustrated by considering the basic good of marriage. As a self-evident reason for action, marriage's nature is such that its realization depends upon a free choice for marriage by those who are eligible to do so: that is, a man and a woman free to make such a choice.[34] We may thus say that the law wrongly violates human autonomy if it attempts to force into marriage those who choose, for example, to cohabit, fornicate occasionally or regularly, or live a celibate life. The free choice for marriage can be made by no one except a man and a woman free to participate in this good.

This does not mean, however, that the law should refrain from encouraging people to enter into marriage who are free to marry and want to do so; for example, by diminishing the incentives for such people to avoid marriage, for while any human being with unimpaired reason can make choices, it is easier to achieve integral liberty if we receive support from other individuals, communities, and the law. Noted liberal scholars have stressed the legitimacy of such support, especially in light of observing what can happen to a society's moral ecology when this support is lacking. William Galston, for instance, has underlined the degree to which the proliferation of certain habits have undermined marriage and the family in Western societies. He has consequently argued that liberals must distance themselves from "the thesis that questions of family structure are purely private matters not appropriate for public discussion and response."[35] This is a considerable concession from a self-identified liberal theorist. It reflects Galston's willingness to include the notion of damage to the moral-cultural order among the harmful acts of persons that ought to be discouraged legally—a notion that many liberal thinkers have hitherto largely ignored or denied.

How then could the law carry out this educative function in ways that do not unjustly infringe personal autonomy? One way would be through its continuing adherence to rules that encourage people to identify, support, and participate in the basic goods, and to discourage people from acting in ways that diminish their self-mastery. Thus, we should not be wary of laws that encourage people to know, for instance, about marriage, why it is a good, and why cohabiting is an error. This does not mean that law should make every act against the basic goods a criminal offence by, for example, jailing cohabitors, nor does it imply that law should confer upon cohabitors any of the civil benefits of marriage. It is therefore entirely possible for law to assist us in our pursuit of integral liberty while avoiding unreasonable intrusion upon our interior acts of free choice.

A useful way of conceptualizing these distinctions is through that much misunderstood term *subsidiarity*. We find this idea partially formulated in Aquinas's thought when he commented that, "It is contrary to the proper character of the State's government to impede people from acting according to their responsibilities—except in emergencies."[36] A fuller and more recent definition of subsidiarity has been articulated in the following terms:

> A community of a higher order should not interfere in the internal life of a community of a lower order, depriving the latter of its functions but, rather, should support it in case of need and help to co-ordinate its activity with the activities of the rest of society, always with a view to the common good.[37]

The interventions of higher communities in the activities of lower bodies ought therefore be made with reference to the common good: that is, the conditions that enable all persons to fulfill themselves. Subsidiarity thus combines axioms of *noninterference* and *assistance*. It follows that when a case of assistance and coordination through law is necessary, as much respect as possible for the rightful autonomy of the person or community being assisted should be preserved.

The significance of this principle thus lies not so much in the autonomy that subsidiarity confers upon people but in the fact that this autonomy is essential if people are to act freely for basic goods. Subsidiarity has therefore less to do with efficiency than with people attaining integral liberty. A basic requirement for realizing this liberty is to act and to do things for ourselves—as the fruit of our own reflection, choices, and acts—rather than to have others do them for us.

The importance of prudence in fleshing out the precise application of law's subsidiary function cannot be underestimated. As the theologian Germain Grisez observes, "In identifying legal crimes, society must have a clear idea of what is and is not wrong." The same society, however, Grisez adds, "also needs to consider what wrong actions should—and should not—be treated as crimes."[38] There are compelling reasons that may lead us to tolerate—as opposed to accept or to endorse—certain actions that decrease people's integral liberty. The law should not therefore seek to prevent any possibility of people acting unreasonably. No doubt that the law could seek to protect the good of truth by forbidding all forms of lying. Yet, prudence suggests that outlawing all forms of lying would necessitate the creation of an all-seeing, all-pervasive State apparatus to enforce such a law. Hence, we prudentially limit law to prohibiting lying in matters such as contracts and court cases and leave it to others to discourage lying in other contexts.

Pluralism and Coercion

One concern likely to be expressed by some liberals is that the view of law articulated in this chapter could unjustly curtail the degree of pluralism that exists in a given society. The legal prohibition of various actions may unduly reduce people's options for choice, and, thus, the diversity present in a given society.

Such fears underestimate the role that coercion can play in assisting people to make autonomous choices that are, in fact, *valuable*. Neither the importance of autonomy nor the value of pluralism is undermined by the fact that acts of stealing are forbidden by the law. Surely coercion that inhibits or prevents non-valuable activities does not deprive anyone of valuable autonomy.[39] Respect for liberty certainly requires law to allow room for choices among different and sometimes incompatible goods. It does not entail, however, that people should be allowed as a matter of *right* to make unreasonable choices.

Nor does this type of coercion damage the opportunities for pluralism that emerge when people recognize that the reality of the basic goods provides us with numerous possibilities for choosing the precise way that we achieve integral liberty.[40] In a lifetime, a person may pursue different goods with different degrees of commitment, and periodically change some of these commitments based upon a prudential assessment of his talents, abilities, and circumstances. A mature adult may, for example, choose to study in his twenties, focus on his work in his thirties, cultivate aesthetic appreciation more systematically as he acquires the means to do so, and deepen his exploration of the ultimate truth about the universe as he grows older. Others may choose different paths to integral liberty by cultivating the same goods in different ways, times, and contexts.

Many of these potential choices for the good may be incompatible with each other. A person cannot simultaneously choose a career as a trial lawyer and pursue a vocation to a cloistered life in a monastery. This does not, however, mean that there are no choices unworthy of human freedom. The fact of different incompatible choices, such as choosing to have dinner with a close friend (the good of friendship) or instead, choosing to use that time to engage in an hour of solitary study (the good of knowledge), does not mean that using the same time to drink oneself into oblivion is an equally valid choice. Clearly the pluralism associated with integral liberty does not require people to aspire to neutrality about the good. It allows great room for choice *without* implying that all choices are reasonable or equally valid.

In a world of ordered pluralism, the role of law becomes more than simply protecting the moral ecology from direct infringement. Law also helps people to acquire integral liberty by (1) minimizing conflicts between reasonable actions, (2) diminishing the possibility of unjust coercion, and (3) reminding us that certain choices are unworthy of human beings. One means by which law fulfills these roles is known as the rule of law.

Practical Reason and Rule of Law

The concept of rule of law is, in the view of liberal and conservative thinkers alike, one of the most vital institutions in a free society. Hayek commented, for example, that "the importance which the certainty of law has for the smooth and efficient running of a free society can hardly be exaggerated. There is probably no single factor that has contributed more to the prosperity of the West than the relative certainty of the law that has prevailed here."[41]

Rule of law is commonly regarded as describing a variety of requirements in the application of law that must be met if such an application is to be considered just. Such principles of natural justice normally include the following characteristics:[42]

- Rules are promulgated and are clear and coherent with respect to each other.
- Rules are prospective rather than retroactive and not impossible to comply with.
- Rules are sufficiently stable to allow people to be guided by their knowledge of the content of the rules.
- Those charged with the authority to make and administer rules are accountable for their own compliance with the rules, and administer the law consistently.
- There is a recognized division of responsibility in administering the law. No one can, for example, be simultaneously judge, witness, public prosecutor, and public defender.

A law can thus be said to treat its subjects seriously when it is promulgated, clear, general, stable and, above all, *practically reasonable*. When a law fails to meet these criteria, rule of law degenerates into "rule of men." An example might be the inconsistent application of the sanctions attached to a law because of a judge's arbitrary whim. Such an act is naturally unjust precisely because it is unreasonable.

By conforming to these principles, law makes a vital contribution to freedom from unjust coercion. Because all of us are subject to the same law, our obedience to the law means that we are not formally subject to the arbitrary will of those wielding legitimate coercive power. *We thus enjoy liberty under law.* This is what Hayek had in mind when he distinguished the rule of law from the rule of men.

If, however, we agree with Aquinas that law is ultimately an ordinance of reason, then law itself is more than just the stability of rules and their consistent application. It is entirely possible for unreasonable laws to be stable and applied consistently by individuals who do not exempt themselves from its requirements. If rule of law is therefore to be just, it evidently requires more solid grounding.

Interestingly, it was Aquinas who first stated that the rule of law is "not the rule of men."[43] By "rule of law," Aquinas did not primarily mean that those charged with administering the law simply upheld established rules and procedures consistently. Rule of law was, for Aquinas, a matter of acting according to *reason:* that is, according to precepts that resulted from man's rational will rather than from our passions. Rule of law does not therefore mean that magistrates are forbidden to exercise their reason when making decisions. Certainly Aquinas believed, like Aristotle, that as far in advance as possible, law should determine in advance what judges should decide.[44] Nonetheless even after laws are promulgated, Aquinas recognized that further exercises of reason are required, not least because many laws inevitably require judges to exercise their judgment to address inevitable ambiguities of meaning, to reconcile different laws, and to fill in gaps in law.

This attention to reasonableness is at the heart of the rule of law. Indeed, when people object to totalitarianism, they are not normally objecting to the power of law or the State per se. They are objecting to coercive power being arbitrarily constituted or exercised, for to treat people inconsistently with an agreed-upon rule—a rule that is coherent, nonarbitrary, efficient, and does not facilitate damage of any of the basic goods—is to act against a basic good: that of practical reasonableness. Maintaining rule of law is thus always dependent on respecting this particular basic good.

Those legal theories described as "positivist" hold that rule of law can be analyzed and explained without reference to such premises. In broad terms, legal positivism insists that the existence of law is ultimately dependent upon social usages and practices that have proved their validity over time rather than upon reasoned discernment of the requirements of practical reasonableness. From the positivist perspective, the expression "rule of law" simply refers to a set of ordinances that have evolved in order to deal with increasingly complicated societies.

Without question, law is shaped by cultural and social practices. This is evident from study of the differences between Anglo-Saxon common law and European codified law. Nonetheless, the very idea of the rule of law is partly derived from the conclusion that it is *reasonable* to limit arbitrary power. Rule of law thus contains a distinct inner morality insofar as arbitrariness is understood to be unreasonable. This underlines the accuracy of Finnis' observation that "the reasons people have for establishing systems of positive law . . . and for maintaining them (against the pull of strong passions and individual self-interest), and for reforming and restoring them when they decay or collapse, include certain moral reasons, on which many of those people often act."[45]

Others, writing from a different jurisprudential perspective, agree. The jurist Lon Fuller insisted, for example, that rule of law incarnates an inner moral logic inasmuch as there are certain conditions of reason that a law must meet before it is understood to be a legitimate law.[46] Unless, for instance, a law is clear and promulgated, it is regarded as unreasonable and therefore unjust. This requirement is not simply a technical precondition for a functioning legal system. It contains an inner reasonableness insofar as these requirements testify that there are just and unjust ways of systematizing social life. Even in situations of tyranny, the formal treatment of citizens with fairness is still good. Not only does it reflect a choice to treat people as reasonable creatures; it also encourages people to reach conclusions concerning the reasonableness of procedures rather than meekly bowing to unjust actions.

Reflection upon the legal procedures that ought to prevail in a regime of ordered liberty soon prompts us to realize that the rule of law is only one of its necessary institutional characteristics. The very prevalence of rule of law in a society suggests that a constitutional order exists inasmuch as it indicates that all acts of State power in a society can be studied, judged, and criticized from the standpoint of natural justice. This is especially important for a society that aspires to be free, for it is through the constitutionally ordered State and the jurisprudence of rights that the coordination of free acts is increasingly rendered throughout the world.

Notes

1. Montesquieu, *The Spirit of the Laws*, I, 3.

2. See Roger Scruton, *The Meaning of Conservatism* (London: Penguin, 1980), 71.

3. See H. L. A. Hart, *The Concept of Law* (Oxford: Oxford University Press, 1961), 202.

4. François Guizot, "Philosophie politique: de la souveraineté," in *Histoire de la civilisation en Europe*, ed. P. Rosanvallon (Paris: Cerf, 1985), 366.

5. Guizot, "Philosophie politique: de la souveraineté," 367.

6. Hayek, *Constitution*, 148.

7. Ibid., 151.

8. For a longer study of this issue, see Joseph Boyle, in "Natural Law and the Ethics of Traditions," in *Natural Law Theory*, 3–30.

9. See Gerald J. Postema, *Bentham and the Common Law* (Oxford: Clarendon Press, 1986).

10. See Hume, *An Enquiry Concerning the Principles of Morals*, 145.

11. See Aquinas, *ST*, I-II, q. 99, a. 2, ad. 2.

12. Aquinas, *ST*, I-II, q. 95, a. 1.

13. Aristotle, *Ethics*, x.9.1179b.

14. Tocqueville, *Democracy*, 274.

15. Mill, *On Liberty*, 9.

16. John Rawls, *Political Liberalism* (New York: Columbia University Press, 1996), xx.

17. Ibid., 61, 127.

18. Ibid., xliv.

19. Ibid.

20. Finnis, "The Catholic Church and Public Policy Debates," 261, fn. 1.

21. See Robert P. George, *The Clash of Orthodoxies: Law, Religion, and Morality in Crisis* (Wilmington, Del.: ISI Books, 2001), 54.

22. William Galston, "Liberalism and Public Morality," in *Liberals on Liberalism*, ed. A. J. Damico (Totowa, N.J.: Rowman and Littlefield, 1986), 183.

23. This critique follows closely that of George in *Making Men Moral*, 83–109.

24. Ronald Dworkin, *Taking Rights Seriously* (Cambridge: Harvard University Press, 1977), 198.

25. Ibid., 273.

26. See George, *Making Men Moral*, 95.

27. John Finnis, "Legal Enforcement of 'Duties to Oneself': Kant v. Neo-Kantians," *Columbia Law Review*, 87 (1987): 437.

28. Ronald Dworkin, *A Matter of Principle* (Cambridge: Harvard University Press, 1985), 349.

29. Ibid., 206.

30. See George, *Making Men Moral*, 98.

31. See Finnis, *Natural Law*, 135–41.

32. See, for example, Aquinas, *ST* I-II, q. 100, a. 9.

33. Hans Kelsen, *The Pure Theory of Law* (Berkeley: University of California Press, 1970), 4.

34. The good of marriage is understood here as a two-in-one-flesh male-female communion of persons consummated and actualized by sexual acts of the reproductive type. For extensive statements of this position, see Robert P. George and Gerard Bradley, "Marriage and the Liberal Imagination," *Georgetown Law Journal*, 84 (1995): 299.

35. William Galston, *Liberal Purposes* (Cambridge: Cambridge University Press, 1991), 285.

36. Thomas Aquinas, *Summa Contra Gentiles* (Notre Dame, Ind.: University of Notre Dame Press, 1997), III, c. 71, n. 4.

37. John Paul II, *Centesimus Annus*, par. 48.

38. Germain Grisez and Russell Shaw, *Fulfillment in Christ: A Summary of Christian Moral Principles* (Notre Dame: University of Notre Dame Press, 2001), 132.

39. See Christopher Wolfe, "Being Worthy of Trust: A Response to Joseph Raz," in *Natural Law, Liberalism, and Morality*, ed. Robert P. George (Oxford: Oxford University Press, 1996), 135.

40. See George, *Making Men Moral*, 189–229.

41. Hayek, *Constitution*, 208.

42. See Finnis, *Natural Law*, 270–73.

43. Thomas Aquinas, *Sententia Libri Ethicorum*, c. 11, n. 10, in *Thomae Aquinatis Opera Omnia*, ed. Busa.

44. Ibid.

45. John Finnis, "The Truth in Legal Positivism," in *The Autonomy of Law: Essays on Legal Positivism*, ed. Robert P. George (Oxford: Oxford University Press, 1996), 204.

46. See Lon Fuller, *The Morality of Law*, 2d ed. (New Haven, Conn.: Yale University Press, 1977), chaps. 2 and 5.

5

Whither the State?

In passing from despotism to liberty, nations cease to have masters, but they are not replaced by servants. They then have leaders in whose hands authority is not demeaning, and who, in accepting the necessity to act for the common good, remain heads of State.

—François Guizot[1]

Perhaps no subject remains as perennially controversial in political discourse as the role of the State. The cluster of views marshaled under the banner of liberalism emerged partly as a critique of classical and medieval concepts of State power. Central to these developments was an often-acute consciousness that the State—and, more specifically, the organs of government and law—is the only institution that may legitimately exercise coercion.

Over time, the State has assumed a variety of guises. The association of the Greek polis with the deities characterizing the pre-Christian world contrasts dramatically with the prevailing liberal democratic view of government and its connection with the idea of human rights. Tocqueville was one of the first to grasp the significance of these transitions for any society that valued liberty. He always reminded people that, even after the disintegration of aristocratic privilege following the French Revolution, the extent of State power remained an essential question, even in democracies.

A significant debt is owed to the decision of many liberal thinkers to focus on how to limit State power. Their research has yielded a rich literature on subjects such as the ability of written and unwritten constitutions to protect individual freedom. Hayek even claimed that protecting individual liberty was always the priority pursued by "the founders of liberal constitutionalism."[2] This overriding concern for autonomy underlies, as observed, the thought of liberal scholars such as Dworkin and Rawls.

In seeking to limit State power constitutionally, liberal theorists have generally avoided making any reference to the good or the truth. Many liberals are also wary of those who aspire to use State power to pursue some greater good. There are sound reasons for this. Such aspirations have in the past been determined and justified by reference to the will of the Revolution (Jacobinism), the *Volk* (Nazism), or the proletariat (Communism). At an even more basic level, Sir Thomas More was surely right to surmise that "unlimited power has a tendency to weaken good minds . . . even in the case of very gifted men."[3]

What, however, liberals have been less willing to consider is that an absence of some reference point beyond choice or preference can open the road to more subtle forms of tyranny. In their concern for liberty, some liberals may have actually placed freedom in danger. The irony is that a commitment to fostering integral liberty within a society may well be an effective way of limiting the State's coercive activities, but without relying upon skepticism as the source of legitimacy for such restrictions.

The State and the Common Good

Defining the limits of State power requires a clear grasp of its purposes. This in turn reflects the fact that human persons rely greatly upon association with others.

From the moment of our conception, we depend upon our mother for sustenance. As a baby, we are helpless, utterly dependent upon the goodwill of others, especially our families. As we grow, however, our associations with others gradually become less exclusively familial. They increasingly become the outcome of human reason and choice. This reflects our condition as a social being whose capacity for self-reliance is limited. No doubt reflecting in part upon his life as a scholar in monasteries and universities, Aquinas highlighted this truth when he wrote:

> It is not possible for one man to arrive at knowledge of all these things by his own individual reason. It is therefore necessary for man to live in a multitude so that each one may assist his fellows, and different men may be occupied in seeking, by their reason, to make different discoveries—one, for example, in medicine, one in this, another in that.[4]

Nor, presumably, did Aquinas imagine that our dependence upon associational life confined to our immediate circumstances. When we engage in shaping material, be it physical or intellectual in nature, we almost always draw upon a common stock of human knowledge. This can range from something as fundamental as language, to a specific technique developed over time by particular professions. In undertaking his project of discerning what in Greek thought was compatible with the Revelation preached by Christianity, Aquinas himself drew on the work of his teachers, such as Albertus Magnus, as well as that of men who lived 1,500 years before him. Like Sir Isaac Newton, Aquinas understood that he stood on the shoulders of giants.

Yet, no matter how apparently trivial or significant they may seem, our associative acts do not always require accord about the end to be achieved. Even the apparently disassociative act of differing with someone as we debate him involves two or more people aligning their respective concepts of an idea in order to determine where and why discrepancy exists.

Many forms of associative action are directed to a common basic good, even if the acts themselves are different. A person at church may choose to *listen* to the priest's sermon in order to deepen his commitment to certain beliefs about the transcendent, but the priest himself has chosen to *speak* the words because he has devoted much of his life to the same good of religion. Moreover, both listener and speaker are engaging their reason in pursuing this good and are thereby involved in intrinsically valuable practical reasoning. We thus see that the basic goods are indeed "common" goods because they may be participated in innumerable ways by infinite numbers of persons.

Not all types of associative action have the same good as their end. There are, for example, what Aristotle called "relationships of utility." In these cases, two or more people agree to observe certain conditions. In their totality, these conditions constitute an instrumental common good that enables all people involved in the relationship to pursue different ends. Two people attending a lecture may, for example, agree to be quiet when the lecturer is speaking: the first because of his choice to assimilate the knowledge imparted by the lecturer; the second because she is painting a portrait of the lecturer.

While families and intermediate associations establish some of the conditions that facilitate our ability to participate in the basic goods, no single community can promote and protect the conditions that assist all people to achieve integral liberty. No single business, for example, no matter how successful, can provide for the widely diverse and reasonable material requirements of any one group of associations or individuals. Likewise, a Church cannot resolve all disputes between individuals and associations, not least because not everyone will recognize the authority of a Church to act in such a manner. The situation is further complicated by the fact that in any one cluster of individuals, families, and associations, there will always be disputes concerning the reasonableness of many actions. Thus, a need exists for some organization to resolve many such disputes in a formal and authoritative manner.

Law is one means by which such coordination may occur. Law itself is not an expression of the will of any one individual or any one group. Even in tyrannical situations, the law is rarely understood, in formal terms, to be the expression of one person's arbitrary decisions. It is normally held to reflect the reasoned will of a wider community that encapsulates many individuals and associations. This wider grouping may be called a *political community* or the *body politic*.

The requirement for such a community becomes more evident as the range of different, sometimes incompatible, possibilities for reasonable choice by individuals and associations continues to expand. It therefore becomes increasingly difficult to reconcile all choices with each other. Decisions thus need to be made concerning the processes, rules, and policies that allow different reasonable choices to be reconciled, and to address problems arising from unreasonable choices.

In certain areas, various procedures emerge to resolve particular problems. By reflecting the supply and demand status of different goods and services, the price mechanism that functions in economic life provides people with some of the information they need in order to choose what to purchase. Nevertheless, even here, judgments need to be made concerning what to do when, for example, a person reneges on his or her promise to pay the agreed-upon price.

When it comes to deciding how to coordinate a multitude of free acts, there are only two ways: unanimity or authority.[5] The agreed, voluntary undertakings contained in a contract, for instance, are based upon unanimity insofar as the contracting individuals adhere to the original voluntary agreement. In the case of a breakdown of unanimity, the two individuals either (1) agree to dissolve the contract (unanimity), or (2) they admit the authority of a law demanding completion of agreed undertakings, or (3) they are held to their undertakings by some organization wielding a recognized authority.[6]

The ongoing increase of possible reasonable and unreasonable choices in most societies decreases the possibility of achieving unanimity on a range of questions. While this may mirror increasing dissension about the proper ends of people, it also reflects an increase in the incompatible but nonetheless reasonable ways of pursuing incompatible but reasonable ends. The subsequent lack of unanimity necessitates:

- a community invested with *authority;*
- the charging of particular institutions (collectively described as *the State*, which in turn embraces the *government* and the *law*) of that community with the responsibility of exercising that authority; and
- the defining and delimiting of the subsequent powers of these institutions.

As a form of human association, the political community may thus be understood as existing to assist all its members to realize integral liberty. Its ways of doing so might include: interacting with other political communities; protecting its members from hostile outsiders; vindicating justice by punishing wrongdoers;

or defining the responsibilities associated with particular relationships, such as contractual duties and the obligations of harm-doers to the harmed.

What these activities have in common is that they are all conditions that *assist*, as distinct from directly *cause*, people to achieve self-mastery. It is harder, for example, to choose to pursue the good of knowledge in a situation of civil disorder. Likewise, we know that the incentives for us to work for someone else will be radically diminished if there is no guarantee that our earnings will not be arbitrarily taken from us.

These conditions thus constitute the common good of a political community. A particular characteristic of this common good is that it is not the all-inclusive end of its members. Rather, it is *instrumental* inasmuch as it is directed to assisting the integral fulfillment of persons.[7] The common good of the political community thus helps not only to define its legitimate authority, but to limit it, for the political community's authority does not derive its power from itself. It always proceeds from the responsibility of State institutions to serve a political community's common good.

Provided that this common good is understood in the terms stated above, liberals have less reason to believe that it will become the basis for authoritarian tendencies. For one thing, the State's responsibility for the political community's common good is to help people to make choices for the basic goods, not to force them to do so. Second, the common good, properly understood, does not necessarily require uniformity. It actually creates room for pluralism insofar as it seeks to enable as many people as possible to pursue the basic goods in a potentially infinite number of ways. Even disagreement among those charged with determining what the State may do in pursuing the common good, does not imply that the common good is not being served. Argument may actually contribute to the common good precisely because beneath the hustle, hyperbole, and rhetoric of political debate, the relevant individuals may be engaging in a serious discussion about the most reasonable means of serving the common good. Such discussion is surely essential if State institutions are to act reasonably.

A Question of Prudence

This understanding of the political community and its common good provides us with the basis for serious reflection upon the principles that determine what State authorities may do in a society that values freedom. Far from constituting an open-ended invitation to expanded government, it actually points us in the direction of limited government. It indicates, for example, that the political community is only one of a number of communities and should not therefore displace or absorb the proper responsibilities of other individuals and associations. Understood in this way, the common good of a political society is incompatible with totalitarianism of any kind, precisely because the totalitarian State attempts to absorb all other groups within itself. Even social welfare measures of modern democratic States must, if they are to serve the political community's common good, be limited to assisting rather than usurping the efforts of others to establish conditions that assist others to help themselves.

The State's ability to perform this assistance role is, however, complicated by a number of factors. One might be called the knowledge problem. Attempting to determine the conditions that constitute a political community's common good is an extremely difficult exercise. The totality of these conditions is never static. Hence, just as one individual cannot know everything, nor can the State authorities know everything about all the conditions that constitute the common good of a political community at any one point in time. Neither legislators nor judges are in a position to know the number and particular character of obligations incumbent upon all individuals and associations. A similar insight lies at the heart of the critique of the Socialist experiment by free-market economists such as Mises and Hayek. They argued that socialism was impossible because it assumed that the State authorities could at any one point know everything about the millions of daily transactions that occur in the economic realm. The slow implosion of Communist economic systems illustrates how accurate Mises and Hayek were.

There are, however, some occasions when a political community's common good requires State institutions to act in an authoritative and often coercive manner, despite the fact that they cannot know everything. This may include, among other things, punishing violations of justice. It may also embrace adjudicating disputes between reasonable courses of action in those instances where they cannot be resolved without the exercise of State authority.

We are thus faced with a dilemma. If we are to flourish as human beings, we need to be able to act under our own volition. Yet, we cannot do so if our decisions are constantly preempted for us by the State. On the other hand, our opportunities for free choice may be unreasonably limited if certain prerequisites such as public order and rule of law, which rely heavily upon State authority for their efficacy, are absent.

This underscores the importance of State institutions and officials cultivating a special type of human wisdom if they are to assume their responsibilities for a society's political common good. This wisdom consists of discerning what the political community can properly and reasonably contribute toward the integral liberty of its members.[8] Aquinas underlined this point when he specified three levels of prudential wisdom: individual *prudentia;* domestic practical reasonableness, and political practical reasonableness. "The good of individuals, the good of families, and the good of *civitas*," he wrote, "are different ends; so there are necessarily different species of *prudentia* corresponding to this difference in their respective ends."[9]

One way of prudentially discerning the role of State institutions in a given situation is to ask ourselves what the State can generally do well and what it cannot. This may be determined by identifying the deficiencies of other groups and asking when no other community, save the State, is able to render the assistance that will remedy the deficiency until the wanting social organization can reassume its appropriate role.

Reason and experience tell us that no family is capable of securing public order or administering justice within a political community. Nor can any private person, local association, or Church successfully undertake such a role. The same reason and experience suggest, however, that the State is a very inadequate child-raiser. In normal circumstances, this function is properly performed by a family that knows and loves its children. When the family experiences problems beyond its control, it should normally be the case that extended family or neighbors are the first to render assistance. When no other group can render the appropriate form of assistance, it may then be necessary for the State to attempt to do so.

Hence, the fact that children are best raised by their families does not rule out, in principle, any possibility of State intervention in particular circumstances. Examples might be when the police are summoned to stop a man beating his wife or when State officials use force to prevent a parent from sexually abusing a child. The urgent need to protect the goods of life and health in such cases may make it imprudent to wait for other family members or other intermediate groups to intervene.

Nonetheless, direct State intervention in family matters is generally unwise because it involves, in part, the application of political wisdom to a sphere where domestic wisdom ought to prevail. The State's responsibility to maintain an order of justice will nevertheless occasionally necessitate such intervention, precisely because failure to act coercively against the wife-beater or child-abuser may contribute to a deterioration of the public order that is essential for a political community's common good. Though it is impossible for the State to prevent all cases of, for instance, stealing and intentional killing, such actions should always be prohibited by State authority. For unless such practices are always discouraged and face the ultimate sanction of State punishment, a fundamental condition that assists all to fulfill themselves will not prevail.

This suggests that, in principle, State institutions may act in ways that contribute to the moral-cultural dimension of a society's common good. The same common good, however, demands that the State should not attempt to protect or alter a society's moral ecology in ways that seek to force people to acquire virtuous dispositions. This point is well explained by Germain Grisez in his reflections on the nature of the political order. Though recognizing that a political community will not be well ordered unless most of its members are encouraged to freely choose acts that lead to integral liberty, Grisez insists that it is not the State's *direct* responsibility to demand virtue in general:

> Even though a political society cannot flourish without virtuous citizens, it plainly cannot be government's proper end *directly* to promote virtue in general ... both the limits of political society's common good and its instrumentality in relation to the good of citizens as individuals and nonpolitical communities set

analogous limits on the extent to which government can rightly concern itself
with other aspects of morality, especially insofar as they concern the interior
acts and affections of heart rather than the outward behavior which directly
affects other people.[10]

While we should expect those exercising State power to act in a virtuous manner,
it is not the State's primary concern to promote virtue directly. The important
word in Grisez's reflection is, however, *directly*. This indicates that the State's
legitimate concern for public order is not limited to upholding the law and pro-
cedurally adjudicating disputes. Rather, it is a question of State institutions indirectly supporting the efforts of individuals to choose the good freely, while
directly fulfilling its responsibility to the common good by addressing those
problems that cannot be resolved through the actions of individuals, families,
and intermediate associations.

Toward Constitutional Order

The need for people to make free choices normally means formally delimiting
the power of State institutions to, unwittingly or otherwise, restrict such choices
unreasonably. A genuine concern that people realize integral liberty means that
the State should only help people in ways that respect their need to be reasonable, to choose, and to act. Thus the way in which State authority functions
becomes subject to the conditions that allow all to achieve integral liberty: that
is, the common good.

If State institutions are to serve the political community's common good,
they need to do so in a reasonable manner. Hence, a division of responsibility
between State organs is required by virtue of the fact that we know that no one
individual can perform all the functions of government. The same concern for
the common good also demands delineation of the limits of each State organ's
coercive powers as well as some specification of the appropriate relationships
between these institutions, for unless such certainty exists, it becomes more difficult for individuals, families, and intermediate associations to make choices in
a reasonably predictable social environment. Concern for the common good thus
gives rise to constitutional order.

Historically speaking, the roots of constitutionalism may be traced to the
ancient Greeks and, particularly, to the Athenians of the fourth and fifth centuries B.C. As an idea, it received powerful systematization in the Middle Ages,
especially in the works of Aquinas, in the internal organization of religious
orders, as well as in the emerging commercial cities of Italy and Germany. Some
rulers were able to minimize the impact of emerging rules for political order, and
thereby exercise a type of absolute rule. Even the Bourbon monarchs of France,
however, found that their efforts to create an absolutist political regime were
limited by the authority of France's regional legal assemblies, known as the *par-*

lements. Likewise, the Hapsburg rulers of the Austrian Empire found themselves compelled to exercise their power through the various constitutions governing different parts of their polyglot realm.

By the seventeenth and eighteenth centuries, philosophers ranging from John Locke to Jean-Jacques Rousseau were expounding the benefits of specific constitutional arrangements. To minimize the potential misuse of power, Charles de Montesquieu, insisted that "it is necessary from the very nature of things that power should be a check to power."[11] He thus sought to separate the process of determining "the general will" of the State from the execution of that general will.

Yet, no matter how influential these contributions to constitutional theory, careful reflection upon the nature of authority in any political community tells us that some type of constitutional order will *always* exist, however rudimentary, often in the form of custom, precedent, and tradition. Even in dictatorships, there is a need to allocate different roles, powers, and responsibilities to different State organs, and to define (however unreasonably) the relationships between them. What distinguishes a dictatorial order from nondictatorial regimes is that the latter's source of authority is not the will or charisma of a Stalin, Idi Amin, Fidel Castro, or Pol Pot. Rather, legitimate State authority is derived from its rational character and the perceived responsibility of institutions charged by the political community to act authoritatively in certain ways, while simultaneously being forbidden to make decisions about other subjects.

Constitutionalism in this sense reflects an effort to establish a *reasonable* relationship between those charged with State authority and those who are not. For the idea of constitutional order is not only about limiting the potential for arbitrary power. It is also implicitly rooted in claims that are reasonable; that, for example, the political community's common good requires some separation of powers. The claims of constitutional authority are thus respected by members of the political community, precisely because they are grounded in reason. The existence of a constitutional order need not therefore be understood as primarily derived from an effort to institutionalize skepticism about the efficacy of State power.

The same concern for reasonableness means that once a constitutional order has been established, there is always a strong prima facie case for adhering to constitutional provisions. Constitutional orders involve all members of a given society undertaking prior obligations to act in particular ways, such as abiding by the legitimate decisions of authority even if one disagrees with that decision. This is perhaps especially true of constitutional democracies. The delegation of authority to elected representatives means that we must be willing to assume that our representatives will debate matters seriously, and that they have taken into account facts concerning the common good of which we may be unaware, precisely because it is their responsibility to make themselves as aware as possible of such facts.

Adherence to constitutional precepts derived from reasoned reflection upon the requirements of the common good is also likely to limit the State authorities' freedom of action and enhance that of citizens. A regime seeking to pursue ends other than the common good has no reason to observe the discipline of acting consistently according to mandated constitutional processes. The very point of such limitations is furtherance of the common good rather than its usurpation.

The same reasoning suggests that, in certain circumstances, we ought to ensure that constitutions provide for the State authorities to act in ways from which they would otherwise abstain. Constitutions do, after all, serve the common good and thus, the continued existence of a political community. They do not oblige a political community to permit its own destruction. In a time of crisis, a constitution must be capable of ensuring that its guidelines for order do not prevent the State from acting against illegitimate attempts to overturn or subjugate the political community. In extraordinary circumstances, such as a civil insurrection, a general strike, or the outbreak of war, it may be in the interests of the common good that particular constitutional canons are temporarily suspended and emergency constitutional provisions prevail until the crisis is overcome. The temporary and selective suspension of habeas corpus, for example, may be necessary if a government is to fulfill its responsibility to halt a terrorist bombing campaign, perhaps by using methods normally considered ultra vires. Provisions for such eventualities ought, therefore, be inscribed into the Constitution. This will give the citizenry good reasons to continue to respect the authority of the relevant State agencies during a crisis, while simultaneously reminding State institutions that their emergency powers are ultimately grounded in and limited by their responsibility to advance the common good—the same common good that requires the government to relinquish such emergency powers when the crisis has passed.

Evolution or Constructivism?

While the approach to constitutions outlined here is likely to result in limiting State power, we should recognize that, unlike many liberal students of constitutionalism, this is not its primary focus. Its main objective is to ensure that the allocation of authority among State institutions meets the demands of reason by serving the common good. The drafting of a constitution is thus an act of reason, but one of a specific kind: an activity of the practical intellect that Aquinas called *determinatio*.[12]

Reason itself requires that those in authority translate a political community's reasonable commitments into some type of authoritative law to be referenced when conflicts emerge. Constitutions are part of what we call positive law, but a special part of the positive law. The American Declaration of Independence, with its explicit statement that all people have the right to life, liberty, and the pursuit of happiness, is a statement of what a particular political community determined to be its fundamental commitments. The U.S. Constitution was, however, an act of *determinatio* insofar as it detailed various rules that attempt to allow all members of that political community to engage these commitments.

Some fundamental commitments can be translated more or less directly into a constitutional provision. Respect for the basic good of life translates clearly into a constitutional protection of innocent life. In other cases, the translation process is not so simple. Though it may be agreed that a separation of powers will serve the common good, the precise way in which the separation should occur is not so evident. A number of different arrangements concerning, for instance, the power of the judiciary vis-à-vis the legislature may be consistent with the reasonable end of separating powers.

In making these determinations, a great deal of political *prudentia* is necessary. Joseph de Maistre once wrote that a constitution is a solution to the following problem: "Given the population, the mores, the religion, the geographic situation, the political circumstances, the wealth, the good and the bad qualities of a particular nation, to find the laws that suit it."[13] Centuries beforehand, the Greek philosopher Solon arrived at a similar conclusion. When asked what is the best form of constitution, he replied, "First, tell me, for what people and for what epoch."[14] In short, though constitutions must meet the demands of reason and serve the common good, some measure of adjustment to certain specific conditions should normally be included as part of one's reasoned deliberation about this good.

Such adjustment is needed more often than recognized. Comparing Mexico and the United States in the nineteenth century, de Tocqueville observed that Mexico had adopted a constitution like that of the United States. Mexico was, however, unable to overcome instability and anarchy. "The Mexicans," de Tocqueville lamented, "wishing to establish a federal system, took the federal Constitution of their Anglo-American neighbors as a model and copied it almost completely. But when they borrowed the letter of the law, they could not at the same time transfer the spirit that gave it life."[15]

Consciousness of these errors has led some liberals to prefer constitutional arrangements that have emerged over time. Hayek, for instance, portrayed the partly unwritten British constitution as reflecting the type of evolutionary development that was preferable to a written text that its drafters hope will eventually be accepted as a constitution by all members of a political community.

The relative long-term stability of the British political order compared to that of Continental European states, not to mention those of Africa and Latin America, lends much credence to Hayek's thesis. It is also true that the rules of a constitution are often interpreted against a background of conventions, habits, and customs that inform how constitutional responsibilities ought to be carried out.

There is, however, a significant weakness in Hayek's argument. Reflecting upon history, the fifteenth-century English jurist Sir John Fortescue commented that it is almost always the case that new regimes emerge following the overturning of the previous political order.[16] The evidence for this is ample. The

American colonies emerged as a nation following their decision to rebel against a political order that, in the view of many colonists, had become tyrannical. The Whig settlement of 1689 in Britain was preceded by a long struggle between Crown and Parliament, a civil war, a foreign invasion, and the eventual deposition of the senior branch of the Stuart dynasty. The Fifth French Republic, inaugurated by General Charles de Gaulle in 1958, followed the collapse of parliamentary rule in the wake of riots in French Algeria and the military's refusal to obey the legitimate civilian government. In each case, the drafting of new constitutional canons, debate over their provisions, and then some manner of approval by the political community legitimized sudden changes to the political order.

Reason thus plays a greater role in the formation of constitutional regimes than Hayek is willing to acknowledge. Such development need not be viewed as an example of what Hayek would call "constructivism": the error of imagining that we can somehow construct a social order as if people were inanimate, unthinking objects. For the application of political *prudentia* is not a matter of abstract reasoning. It requires the quality of what Aristotle called statesmanship: a statesmanship that integrates consciousness of historical circumstances with the need for individuals to make free choices, and the equally pressing necessity for a social order that allows people to make such choices; a statesmanship that can resist not only arbitrary opinion but also the potential tyranny of majority desires. As the doyen of eighteenth-century German philosophers, Immanuel Kant, put it: "A constitution achieves the greatest possible freedom by framing the laws in such a way that the freedom of each can coexist with the freedom of all."[17]

A prominent feature of modern constitutional orders is their increasing attention to the expression of what are called "rights." The 1789 French Declaration of the Rights of Man and the Citizen proclaims, for example, "Any society in which rights are not securely guaranteed and the separation of powers is not determined, has no constitution." Questions, however, persist concerning the efficacy of the concept of human rights for furthering constitutional order within a political community, for, despite their omnipresence in modern political discourse, it is often unclear just what a right *is*.

Rights and Rights-Talk

While the idea of rights enjoys considerable lineage in theological, philosophical, and legal thought, its promotion received particular impetus from nineteenth-century liberal intellectuals. Tocqueville wrote, for example, that, "Next to virtue as a general idea, nothing, I think, is so beautiful as that of rights, and indeed the two ideas are mingled. The idea of rights is nothing but the conception of virtue applied to the world of politics."[18] Employing somewhat less enthusiastic language, Constant emphasized the necessity of rights for protecting individuals from potential State infringements upon liberty. "There is," he insisted, "a part of human existence which by necessity remains individual and independent, and which is, by right, outside any social competence. At the point where independence and individual existence begin, the jurisdiction of sovereignty ends. If society oversteps this line, it is as guilty as the despot who has, as his only title, his exterminating sword."[19]

The recognition of rights by the State does appear to have the potential to resolve some of the problems of living in a pluralist society. The religious believer, for example, will regard the right of religious liberty as reflecting and protecting his freedom to fulfill his duties toward God. Nevertheless, the same juridical protection of religious liberty as a right means that the nonbeliever cannot be forced to worship anyone or anything. *Thus, the same civil recognition of a right of religious liberty confers upon believer and nonbeliever alike certain protections from State coercion, regardless of their actual beliefs.*

Those, however, who have spoken the language of rights also include people not immediately identifiable as liberal. They embrace the American Founders and Charles de Gaulle, but also the architect of French revolutionary terror, Maximilien Robespierre, and the builder of gulags, Joseph Stalin. This disparity suggests two things: One is that the language of human rights is the most available discourse for universal deliberation about what people are objectively owed in entitlements and protections. The second is that the same language is open to being co-opted by tyrannical regimes to serve unreasonable ends.

Further complicating matters is the fact that despite being among the strongest proponents of rights, liberal thinkers have not proved very adept at providing coherent explanations of their basis. Robert P. George goes so far as to claim that no *secular* thinker has provided "any plausible account of where rights come from or why we should respect others' rights."[20] The legal obligation to respect rights has been formally recognized by most States since the 1948 United Nations Declaration of Human Rights. Yet, as one of the members of the Declaration's drafting committee stated at the time, "We are unanimous about these rights on condition that no one asks why."[21] It seems that the participants decided that agreement on common principles—a common philosophy—was unlikely to be achieved.

Part of the difficulty is derived, as the English philosopher Elizabeth Anscombe illustrated, from the apparent inability of modern philosophy to provide a moral account of anything insofar as it declines to—and cannot—identify an ultimately authoritative source of moral goodness.[22] One need only think of all the unsuccessful modern attempts to establish a foundation for rights. These include the decree of the king; a majority vote in parliament; or, perhaps most strangely, John Rawls' imaginary social contract that abstract nonexistent persons might adopt in an equally imaginary original position. A similar difficulty manifests itself in one of the more famous responses to Rawls' *Theory of Justice.* The first and fundamental proposition of Robert Nozick's 1974 treatise, *Anarchy, State, and Utopia,* is that "individuals have rights," but nowhere in the entire text is there any justification or explanation of this claim. Nozick himself states, "It is

only a minor comfort to note that we here are following the respectable tradition
of Locke, who does not provide anything remotely resembling a satisfactory
explanation of the status and basis of the law of nature in his *Second Treatise*."[23]
Unfortunately, when it comes to matters as serious as rights, we cannot simply
defer to respectable scholarly tradition.

Like David Hume, Constant sought to provide an explanation for rights by
contending that people had those rights that a given society could afford to confer on them.[24] This is a troubling proposition. If rights are understood primarily
in terms of whatever has been authorized by the political community, then their
coherence and stability becomes questionable, for once one accepts that rights
have no stronger foundation than the State's exercise of its sovereign powers,
they may be diminished or even abolished by another act of sovereignty on the
State's part. In such circumstances, rights would simply be identified or abolished according to whatever a particular majority in a particular country at a particular time preferred rights to be. The capacity of constitutions to withstand
such arbitrariness is not infinite.

The lack of a coherent reference point for rights beyond majority preference
thus has more than academic implications. It allows the question of right and
wrong—and therefore of truly inalienable rights—to be replaced by the question
of who has power or a determination to acquire power. Without an authoritative
foundational reference point, any person inevitably becomes endowed with as
much authority to determine rights as another. In these circumstances, we can
still say that a person has a right to privacy or a right to life, but in a world where
preference rather than reason is regnant, people who want to kill life or violate
privacy can offer the blunt retort: "What gives you the authority to prescribe
what is good for me? Why is your preference for life or privacy more significant
than my preference to kill life or violate privacy?"

Rights and the Good

To see rights as safeguards of liberty undermined in the name of preferences
masquerading as rights would surely be one of the cruelest paradoxes of all.
Where, then, do we find the type of foundations that allow us to overcome these
modern problems of rights, but in a way consistent with a commitment to integral liberty?

Much contemporary rights-talk centers around the presumed existence of an
association between two people. To this extent, recognition of a right means that
someone has a duty to another. Others, however, are unsure if this tells us very
much. The jurist Lloyd Weinreb comments "That there is a connection between
rights and responsibilities is, I think, intuitively obvious, but any such intuition
fails to disclose its source."[25]

The key to discovering such a source may be to remember that to respect
human rights is to respect what man *is:* an embodied creature with reason and

free will, capable of making choices that lead to integral liberty. We also know that if people are to have any possibility of realizing this self-mastery, they require certain things. Once we establish that a certain protection or entitlement is essential for any person if he is to have any possibility of realizing integral liberty, we may speak of this protection or entitlement, this essential condition, as a right.

If this is true, then we can say that rights are a way of describing basic elements of the common good. Careful examination of the United Nations Declaration of Human Rights demonstrates that this may indeed be the case.[26] Here we find that the idea of rights normally spoken of in two ways:

1. "Everyone has the right to . . ."; and
2. "No one shall be . . ."

Both expressions are linked to each other inasmuch as the second phrase specifies the limits on the rights arising from the first. Thus, we may say that everyone has a "right to free speech," but also that "no one shall defame another's reputation." The right to free speech is thus inalienable, though subject to the duty that we owe to others not to defame their reputation.

There are variations in the way that "no one shall" statements are expressed. Article 9 of the Declaration of Human Rights notes that "No one shall be subject to arbitrary arrest, detention, or exile." To arrest a person, then, is not unthinkable. Indeed, a person *may* be arrested, provided that due process is followed and his other rights are not unduly infringed. Some of those rights may be found in other parts of the Declaration. Article 10, for example, states: "Everyone is entitled in full equality to a fair and public hearing by an independent and impartial tribunal, in the determination of his rights and obligations and of any criminal charge against him."

Nonetheless, the same Declaration speaks of certain rights that are apparently not only inalienable but *absolute* inasmuch as no qualifying phrase is evident. Article 4 states that "No one shall be held in slavery or servitude; slavery and the slave trade shall be prohibited in all its forms." In this case, there is no room for compromise. For such rights, such as the right not to be intentionally deprived of one's life, reflect the basic goods such as life that are integral to man's very identity. These, we may say, are absolute rights, inasmuch as they reflect a *determinatio* of what Finnis calls "the literally immeasurable value of human personality in each of its basic aspects (the solid core of the notion of human dignity)."[27]

If we examine all the inalienable and absolute rights listed in the Declaration of Human Rights, we see that Finnis makes an important point when he states that they amount to a outline of a political community's common good.[28] In short, they describe those conditions that must prevail in a political community if all people in that society are to be able to choose freely to participate in the basic goods that lead to integral liberty.

The concept of rights as essential features of the common good acquires further credence once we recognize how violating a person's rights damages the political community's common good. If, for example, a person's right to life is intentionally violated by another's choice to kill that individual, the common good is undermined. The damage consists of undermining the confidence of others in that society that the safety of their life is relatively guaranteed. Without such a condition, people will be afraid to work or engage in more than superficial relationships with others. Public order is thus subverted. Such circumstances, in turn, severely hinder our ability to make free choices of a range of reasonable options.

Many liberals will have great difficulty accepting this account of rights. While many liberals are prepared to speak of rights, rather fewer are willing to speak of absolute rights, and even fewer are willing to concede the existence of absolute goods. Hayek, for example, wrote:

> However much we dislike it, we are again and again forced to recognize that there are no truly absolute values whatsoever. Not even human life itself. This again and again we are prepared to sacrifice, and must sacrifice, for some other higher value, even if it be only one life to save a large number of other lives.[29]

Though Hayek at no point indicates what these higher values might be (unless he is assuming that progress is its own justification), his reasoning here is essentially utilitarian: that an unknown number of other lives is always worth more than one—no matter if the other lives involved are Caligula and the Marquis de Sade, and the one life is an innocent child.

There is nothing new about this way of proceeding. The Gospel of John records the high priest Caiaphas's asking the question, "Is it not better than one innocent man be put to death than the whole people perish?"[30] Or, to cite Maximilien Robespierre, "Because *la patrie* must live, Louis must die."[31] Both Robespierre and Caiaphas, in effect, made quantitative judgments about something that cannot be quantified: the worth of one life measured against the lives of a number of others.[32]

Liberals need to understand that statements about rights can only be defended in terms of the duties that give rise to them and a coherent explanation of where these duties come from: that is, respect for the basic goods innate to us as humans. Moreover, once liberals begin to speak of rights as elements of the political community's common good, they will be in an immeasurably better position to demonstrate that the protection of rights by the State is *reasonable*. In such a situation, the role of the State could not be perceived as simply conferring the legal status of rights upon the preferences of a particular group. Rather, to paraphrase Abraham Lincoln, the State would simply declare the right so as to help ensure its legal recognition as quickly as possible in a given society's circumstances.[33] The very act of recognition helps to establish the conditions that assist us to participate in the goods intrinsic to man.

A Right to Do Wrong?

What, then, does this vision of rights imply for the common liberal contention that, provided our act does not harm others, we have "a right to do wrong?"

If rights are both derived from and serve to protect and promote basic goods, then we cannot claim to have a right to choose to act directly against basic goods. The possibility of integral liberty depends upon significant good options being available for rational choice and action. It does not follow, however, that various choices against the basic goods should be protected from *any* form of State prohibition by being given the status of a right.

People may argue, of course, about the prudence of actively prohibiting particular choices. We are not, however, arguing about the prudence: We are arguing about *the principle*. The question of whether a particular choice is indeed a right, and the issue of whether the State may legislate against certain actions are quite different matters. We may well conclude that it would not be prudent, for a variety of good reasons, for the State to legislate on a large number of options for choice. This need not, however, mean that a right has been recognized.

Nonetheless, while it is unreasonable to act in ways that facilitate one's own inner disintegration, every person's need to make free choices should make some such acts immune from State prohibition. A good way of discerning whether the State should prohibit people from acting upon certain choices is to assess their meaning for the common good.

A patient with a terminal illness may choose, for example, to ask a doctor to help him or her commit suicide because of the great pain the patient anticipates enduring. Some who would dispute the reasonableness of such an appeal would nonetheless maintain that the doctors be permitted to accede to the request, as they believe that it is imprudent for the State to intervene in such matters. Surely, however, the direct damage of such a choice to some essential conditions of a political community's common good—such as the reasonable confidence that we all require that our lives will not be intentionally killed by another; the prospect that the nonnegotiable principle of the sanctity of life will be imperceptibly subverted by the rather slippery and deeply utilitarian-influenced idea of "quality of life"; the necessary involvement of a member of a profession ostensibly dedicated to healing human health and preserving life in an intentional act of killing—is a more compelling reason for the State to prohibit any such act of assistance.

This approach allows us to speak of what might be called a "modified harm principle": *Those who want to act in ways that directly damage the common good or directly damage the basic goods need to demonstrate why, beyond the desire to choose, their actions should be permitted.* Precisely how this principle would apply in different circumstances is another subject. Nonetheless, it may be one way of beginning a fresh discussion about the limits of State power that avoids the discussion-stopping non sequitur that the fact of choice is somehow sufficient justification for almost any choice. The correct ends of human actions simply cannot be derived from the idea of choice alone.

Given the intimate relationship between the State, the political common good, and rights, one might conclude that the State bears direct responsibility for protecting all the rights at the core of the political common good. This assumption is unwarranted. By definition, families and intermediate associations precede the State inasmuch as they directly provide most of the conditions that assist people to achieve integral liberty. Hence, they also have a responsibility to safeguard people's rights.

We should, however, recognize that even acceptance of a constitution does not eliminate the potential for conflict between State institutions and the intermediate associations that have, at least since the eighteenth century, been termed "civil society." Indeed, a political community's precise character will be profoundly influenced by the existence and nature of what some people call its "civil society." This is especially true of the democratic political communities so closely associated with the call for liberty since the late eighteenth century. Tocqueville was one of the first to realize that the quality of a democracy depends radically on the nature and quality of civil associations, not least because they can assist preventing such societies from slowly succumbing to what he called "soft despotism."

Notes

1. François Guizot, *Des moyens de gouvernement et d'opposition dan l'état actuel de la France* (Paris: Nouvelle Cité, 1921), 168.

2. Friedrich Hayek, "The Constitution of a Liberal State," in *New Studies in Philosophy, Politics, Economics, and the History of Ideas* (Chicago: University of Chicago Press, 1978), 98.

3. Thomas More, *The Complete Works of Saint Thomas More*, vol. 3.2, *The Latin Poems*, ed. Clarence H. Miller, Leicester Bradner, Charles A. Lynch, and Revilo P. Oliver (New Haven, Conn.: Yale University Press, 1984), no. 19, 90–91.

4. Thomas Aquinas, *De Regimine principum ad regem Cypri* (Taurini: Marietti, 1948), I, 6.

5. See Finnis, *Natural Law*, 231–33.

6. Ibid., 232.

7. Cf. Aquinas, *SCG*, III c. 80, nn. 14, 15.

8. See John Finnis, "Public Good: The Specifically Political Common Good in Aquinas," in *Natural Law and Moral Inquiry: Ethics, Metaphysics, and Politics in the Work of Germain Grisez*, ed. Robert P. George (Washington, D.C.: Georgetown University Press, 1998), 186.

9. Aquinas, *ST*, II-II, q. 48, a. un.

10. Grisez, *Living a Christian Life*, 850 (emphasis added).

11. Montesquieu, *Spirit of the Laws*, II, 4.

12. Aquinas, *ST*, I-II, q. 95, a. 2.

13. Maistre, *Considerations on France*, 53.

14. Solon, *Solonos nomoi*, ed. Eberhard Ruschenbusch (Wiesbaden: Steiner, 1966).

15. Tocqueville, *Democracy*, 165.

16. See Sir John Fortescue, *De Laudibus Legum Angliae*, ed. and trans. Stanley B. Chrines (Cambridge: Cambridge University Press, 1949), c. 12.

17. Immanuel Kant, *Critique of Pure Reason* (London: Dent, 1993), II, i.1.

18. Tocqueville, *Democracy*, 238.

19. Constant, *Political Writings*, 177–78.

20. George, *The Clash of Orthodoxies*, 18.

21. Germain Thils, *Droits de l'homme et perspectives chrétiennes* (Louvain-la-neuve: Fayard, 1981), 51.

22. See G. E. Anscombe, "Modern Moral Philosophy," *Philosophy*, 33 (1958): 11.

23. Robert Nozick, *Anarchy, State, and Utopia* (New York: Basic Books, 1974), 9.

24. See Benjamin Constant, *Les Principes de politique de Benjamin Constant*, ed. Ètienne Hoffman, vol. 1 (Geneva: Seuil, 1980), 60–61.

25. Lloyd Weinreb, "Natural Law and Rights," in *Natural Law Theory*, 286.

26. For a fuller outline of this argument and its use of the Declaration of the Human Rights, see Finnis, *Natural Law*, 210–30.

27. Finnis, *Natural Law*, 225.

28. Ibid., 214.

29. Hayek, "Socialism and Science," in *New Studies*, 298.

30. John 11:50.

31. Cited in J. M. Thompson, *Robespierre* (Oxford: Oxford University Press, 1939), 299.

32. There are rare occasions in which a person may have to make a decision that he or she foresees, but does not intend, will have the side effect of resulting in the death of others. The intention and object of Colonel Claus von Stauffenberg's attempt to assassinate Hitler was to facilitate the opportunity for Germans to overthrow a criminal regime by their own efforts. Hitler's death was a foreseen but unintended result of the only act that would allow such circumstances to be effected. Taken as a general principle, however, the reasoning of Caiaphas and Hayek reflects an effort to measure the immeasurable.

33. See Abraham Lincoln, "Speech at Springfield, Illinois (26 June 1857)," in *The Collected Works of Abraham Lincoln*, vol. 2, ed. Roy Basler et al. (New Brunswick, N.J.: Rutgers University Press, 1953), 405–6.

6

Little Platoons

Each body and each community of citizens retains the right to administer its own affairs, a right which we do not assert to be part of the primitive constitution of the Kingdom, for it dates back further: It is a right of nature and of reason.
—Lamoignon de Malesherbes

As a magistrate of the *noblesse de robe* of *ancien régime* France, Chrétien Guillaume de Lamoignon de Malesherbes was famed for his denunciations of what he viewed as despotic acts of the royal administration. It would be a mistake, however, to view Malesherbes as a precursor to Maximilien Robespierre. In 1792, Malesherbes volunteered, despite his advanced age, to act as King Louis XVI's defense counsel when the French National Convention reluctantly permitted the dethroned monarch legal representation. For his efforts, Malesherbes was guillotined in 1794.

The shock of the violence unleashed by the *ancien régime*'s collapse has always darkened the transition that the French Revolution marks between the aristocratic and democratic worlds. It especially weighed upon Malesherbes' great-grandson, Alexis de Tocqueville. His writings are pervaded by an acute consciousness of the fate of his relatives who played little-to-no-role in *ancien régime* politics, only to perish at the hands of the Jacobin terror. Much of de Tocqueville's life was spent wrestling with the question of how to preserve the best of 1789 while exorcising its barbarous side. In the end, de Tocqueville was

89

not sure that such a project could succeed. Much depended upon the path taken by democratic man in the new post-Revolutionary conditions.

The close association of democracy with various constitutional orders that purport to value freedom inevitably forces us to assess democracy's potential to enhance each person's realization of integral liberty. For while democracy holds much promise for contributing to such an end, the very mildness of democracy brings with it a range of new problems.[1] This is especially true in terms of the stability and vitality of that range of intermediate associations between the family and the State often collectively described as "civil society." François Guizot once wrote that "The idea and fact of society both imply the idea and the fact of government."[2] He may, however, have underestimated the democratic State's capacity to engulf the very society that it exists to serve.

Liberty or Democracy?

Though democracy is commonly linked with modern liberalism, not all liberals have entertained entirely benign views of democracy. Toward the end of his life, Hayek was "profoundly disturbed by the rapid decline of faith in [democracy],"[3] a crisis of confidence in which he appears to have shared. His particular concerns were several. One was that democracy's primary meaning had been transformed from a procedure for making governmental decisions, into a general demand for equality in all things. The second was a more typical classical liberal worry about the potential for democracy's majoritarian principle to become a form of tyranny.

Despite these problems, Hayek defended the democratic method as "the only method of peaceful change of government yet discovered." Democracy, Hayek stated, was a paramount but negative value, "comparable to sanitary precautions against the plague, of which we are hardly aware while they are effective, but the absence of which may be deadly."[4] Interestingly, Sir Isaiah Berlin's espousal of democracy also conveys a sense of resignation rather than of enthusiasm. Democracy, Berlin insisted, on the whole provides a better guarantee of negative freedom, but only on the whole.[5]

While the respective merits of Berlin and Hayek's positions may be discussed on their own terms, both ignore the opportunities that democratic procedures allow for human flourishing, especially in comparison to other systems. In both the ancient and aristocratic worlds, it was not enough to be human for one's essential freedoms to be recognized. The definition, for example, of a citizen in the Greek *polis* depended partly upon the subjugation of the slave.

The compelling moral claim of modern democracy is that it is based on justice insofar as it allows all adults to participate in making the political community's decisions. The democratic maxim is that of consent: No law is valid unless *my* representatives have consented to it.

By opening political participation to all adults, democracy creates a number of opportunities for people to pursue basic goods. Democratic regimes invariably embody procedures that allow all citizens to choose to contribute to the selection of their political representatives. This may encourage some people to reflect upon the demands of the common good, and thus engage in an act of intrinsically valuable practical reasoning. Likewise, participation in democratic processes may help people to identify their own interests in new ways, so that, in de Tocqueville's words, an enlightened regard for themselves constantly begins to prompt them to assist one another and inclines them willingly to sacrifice a part of their time and prosperity to others.[6] Democracy thus encourages people to transcend their immediate interest in the political sphere and to be concerned for others for their own sake in a way that monarchy or oligarchy cannot.

One hastens to add, however, that democracy need not necessarily facilitate such ends. The principle of consent, for example, is silent on the subject of the proper ends of action. Hence, if democratic processes are understood in terms of a will detached from reasoned reflection about the oughts of human action, they may well undermine some of the conditions that constitute the political common good.

To have faith in democracy is therefore to trust in man's capacity to act reasonably. This involves hoping that the majority of people in a political community will continue to use their practical reason to discern what is good for all. For all its problems, a truly self-governing democratic society does offer a noble prospect for enhancing the conditions that assist human flourishing.

This last point is especially important because democracy also embodies a certain temptation to mediocrity.[7] Paradoxically, this is closely associated with the social mobility characteristic of democracy. The dominant passion of *homo democraticus*, de Tocqueville observed, is the desire to overcome inequality. Unfortunately, love of democracy tends to become love of equality, sometimes at the cost of conditions that assist all to fulfill themselves.

The Passions of Equality

As de Tocqueville gazed into the future, he did not view the approach of progressive equality with unambiguous approval. Instead, he was filled with a sense of "religious dread."

> Democratic peoples always like equality, but there are times when their passion for it turns to delirium. . . . It is no use pointing out that freedom is slipping from their grasp while they look the other way; they are blind, or rather they can see but one thing to covet in the whole world.[8]

Though de Tocqueville insisted that the democratic revolution was ultimately driven by the Christian belief in the equality of all people in God's sight, he appears to have perceived a type of communal angst in democratic majorities that drove them to seek to equalize all things, even if this meant behaving despotically.

The democratic State does, after all, seek to uphold the supremacy of the majority's will in an institutionalized manner, whatever the content of that will might happen to be. In democracies, government actions have no legitimacy apart from the will of individuals who compose the political community, whose will is manifested in elections and then enacted by a government representing those who willed them to power.

There is thus a tension in the liberal democratic project between its respect for popular sovereignty and its concern for individual liberty. One proposal commonly advanced for resolving this is to favor representative democracy over direct democracy. The representative approach is regarded as limiting the potential for untrammeled majoritarianism while simultaneously allowing the citizenry to be involved in public decision making. Tocqueville, however, was dubious as to whether the ethos of representative government would prevail. "It is really the people who lead," he stated, "and even though the form of government is representative, it is obvious that the opinions, prejudices, interests, and even the passions of the people can find no lasting obstacles that prevent them from making themselves felt in the daily direction of society."[9]

The sheer force of public opinion in democracy thus leads many people to trust in the judgment of the public at large. Strangely enough, the substance of what the majority propose is often less important that the fact that it is supported by a majority. This can lead to a dangerous abdication of individual judgment. Individuals may start to lose confidence in their own ability to make judgments, especially if their reason leads them to conclusions differing from the democratic consensus.

At this point, we begin to see how democracy can begin to undermine our will to pursue integral liberty. Observing democratic society, de Tocqueville believed that "the will of man is not shattered, but softened, bent, and guided. Men are seldom forced to act, but they are constantly restrained from acting."[10]

This "soft despotism," as de Tocqueville called it, would emerge as the democratic State sought to assure people their material comforts in return for their essentially unconditional support. It would be a mistake, however, to describe such despotism as a form of assistance as it is not concerned with preparing people for integral liberty. Rather, its distinctiveness is a centralization of power that increasingly diminishes our willingness to make genuinely free choices. The consequences for integral liberty are disastrous. In an exasperated tone, de Tocqueville lamented:

> What good is it to me, after all, if there is an authority always busy to see the tranquil enjoyment of my pleasures and going ahead to brush all dangers from my path without giving me even the trouble to think about it, if that authority, which protects me from the smallest thorns on my journey, is also the absolute master of my liberty and my life? If it monopolizes all activity and life to such an extent that all around it must languish when it languishes, sleep when it sleeps, and perish if it dies.[11]

One of de Tocqueville's intellectual heirs, the French political philosopher Pierre Manent, observes that in predemocratic societies, different social associations and castes provided cultural and institutional settings for the development of a variety of moral characteristics that militated against soft despotism. The nobility, the peasantry, commercial guilds, and the clergy gave rise respectively to military courage, stoicism, prudence, and a sense of the transcendent.[12]

The paradox is that a democratic society's long-term stability may depend more upon the existence of similar "virtue-incubators" than we realize. It is a nonsense, James Madison maintained, to imagine that a free political community can survive without citizens who pursue lives of virtue.[13] When free societies began to emerge in the West, the existence of certain widespread moral habits was taken for granted. Powerful personal efforts by individuals to temper their passions made possible democratic institutions.[14]

The demise of the predemocratic order, Manent notes, means that these habits of action have slowly lost a type of natural institutional home, and more the direct subject of individual choice. On one level, this allows more people more opportunities to participate in a variety of goods. Yet the preservation of specific associational settings (many of which reflect distinctions between people, such as occupational differences) for such goods will also become a more difficult exercise in democracies that succumb to an all-conquering passion for equality and view difference as a threat to equality.

Resisting Soft Despotism

Tocqueville's concerns about democracy's potential effects upon a society's moral ecology put him at odds with many fellow nineteenth-century French liberals. Like de Tocqueville, Constant noted that private life in modern societies was becoming a greater preoccupation than public affairs.[15] Constant regarded this as a manifestation of increasing liberty. Tocqueville, by contrast, was pessimistic about the effects of this isolation of citizens from each other. A socially atomized society, he believed, was much less capable of forming the associational bonds that allow people to restrict unwarranted extensions of State power.

Part of de Tocqueville's proposition for preempting soft despotism was the cultivation of a plethora of free associations between the State and individual persons. The activities of these groups—what Edmund Burke famously described as "little platoons"—would help to repair the social links damaged by the ongoing democratic demand for submission to the majority. The same plurality of self-organized and interactive associations would teach people how to engage with others outside their families and help them to acquire the moral habits required by citizens in a democratic order, especially if this society was not to be obsessed with equalizing everything. This would eventually facilitate the emergence of what de Tocqueville called "the independent eye of society" to inform and moderate democratic processes.

A paradoxical example of the importance of an active non-State associational sector for limiting the reach of State institutions is *ancien régime* France. French Enlightenment thinkers commonly viewed its plethora of caste-based associations, duties, and traditions as obstacles to efficiency and utility. "It is important," Rousseau wrote, "in order to state the general will that there exist no partial associations within the State."[16]

No doubt, many such associations did create impediments to efficiency and a determination of the nation's will, but they also personalized and tempered interactions between individuals of all classes and professions. Moreover, it was the existence of these associations that meant that, for all its absolutist tendencies, the *ancien régime* was sometimes better at protecting human freedom than its revolutionary heirs.[17] Between 1 July 1789 and 26 October 1795, France's National Assembly, Legislative Assembly, and National Convention passed a collective total of 15,479 laws in the pursuit of liberty, equality, and fraternity. Yet, by 1795, French society was arguably further away from attaining these ends than before the Revolution. Liberty was deeply constrained; fraternity was a myth; and the inequality of castes had been replaced by the dominance of those members of the middle class—the *notables*—who had profited from the pillaging of Church and aristocratic property. The paradox of the French Revolution was that, in the name of liberty, it destroyed those organizations that had limited the Bourbon monarchy's absolutist tendencies, thus producing an even less free political community. On 14 June 1791, France's National Assembly went so far as to pass a law that had the specific objective of destroying all intermediate associations and organizations in French society. Its preamble read:

> There are no longer corporations in the State; there is no longer anything but the particular interest of each individual, and the general interest. It is permitted to no one to inspire an intermediary interest in citizens, to separate them from the public interest by a spirit of corporation.[18]

Such a law left the individual naked against an all-conquering General Will, be it defined by Enlightenment *philosophe*, Jacobin terrorist, or militaristic Bonapartist.

Rethinking Civil Society

Though associations play a critical role in constraining State power, they also provide numerous opportunities for human flourishing that exist at a nonpolitical, nonfamilial level by helping people to participate in the basic goods. It was with good reason that de Tocqueville warned, "The morals and intelligence of a democratic people would be in as much danger as its commerce and industry if ever a government wholly usurped the place of free associations."[19] It is not enough that we often receive from others. Integral liberty requires that we act, and that others help us to do so.

Given the limits of our specific abilities, circumstances, and beginnings, it is practically reasonable to give priority to those commitments that reflect our most immediate responsibilities. These are generally found in our familial and associational realms. In such associations, people are able to participate in particular basic goods, such as friendship, in ways that are harder to actualize at the more distant level of the political community.

A legitimate question arises, however, concerning the *type* of intermediate communities and associations prevailing in a given society, for the culture of a society's intermediate associations has profound implications for their ability to promote integral liberty.

Until the mid-eighteenth century, the phrase "civil society" was used by legal and political philosophers in two ways: The first was to distinguish the secular realm from that of the ecclesiastical. The second was to denote a political association whose members were subject to the laws of that community. "Civil society" was, in fact, a synonym for what we have described as the political community or the State. Aquinas spoke, for example, of *communitas civilis sive politica*, while John Locke referred to "civil or political society." Indeed, the coterminous use of the expressions "political society" and "civil society" forms part of a European tradition traceable back through mediaeval thinkers to Cicero's idea of *societas civilis*, as well as to Aristotle's notion of civil society as the community, the *polis*, that encapsulated all families and other forms of association.[20]

The concept began to undergo significant change, especially in French and Scottish intellectual circles, in the second half of the eighteenth century. The Physiocrats used the term *société naturelle*, meaning economic relations, to distinguish their area of interest from *société politique*. Likewise, the Scottish Enlightenment scholar, Adam Ferguson, stated that the survival and progress of a civilized social order requires the development of social associations that enjoyed certain protections from State power.

But while Ferguson did not break away from the classical understanding of civil society, he did begin a shift away from it by effectively advocating the development of a *civil* society "within" civil or political society. Hegel, however, initiated the split. He distinguished "the political community" from "civil society"—the latter being understood as those associations within the political community where people pursued their own interests.[21] By the nineteenth century, a range of thinkers, including de Tocqueville and Marx, were employing "civil society" to describe a historically produced sphere of activity between the State and the family.

Their views, however, about the precise nature and value of this intermediate world differed. Tocqueville defined *société civile* as consisting of a range of economic and noneconomic associations. Marx and Engels understood civil society primarily as the sphere of economic activity associated with the evolution of productive relations toward a bourgeois-dominated society: "The State, the political order, is the subordinate," Engels insisted, "and civil society, the realm of economic relations, the decisive element."[22] While de Tocqueville believed that civil society ought to be bolstered to protect freedom from State despotism, Marx wanted to crush it in the name of proletariat liberation.

Another common theme associated with changes in thought about civil society was attention to the spread of commercial relations. While merchant activity predated the various Enlightenments, feudalism's erosion was partly fueled by the expansion of commerce in the High Middle Ages. This promoted a multiplication of wants as well as more complex divisions of labor. It also facilitated the growth of a range of new intermediate groups that were not based on caste. Members of these groups were more mobile and, by definition, more economically independent of feudal structures.

The radical effects of the spread of commerce upon the social order were twofold: First, it allowed people to be increasingly linked to one another without always enjoying a common life, save what was voluntarily entered into by contract. Second, it encouraged people to distinguish between roles and persons. This meant that people could compare roles, and, theoretically at least, aspire to any role.[23]

Awareness of the important change wrought in society by the emergence of market competition and a commercial class profoundly affected the way that Ferguson, Hegel, Marx, and de Tocqueville understood civil society. Economic-centered explanations are, however, surely too simplistic. They neglect the fact that, as observed by the political theorist John Keane, the shift in thinking about civil society was heavily influenced by individuals from distinctly noncommercial backgrounds. Changes in thinking about civil society were also driven by a *political* occurrence: the rise of despotism and the desire to avert it.[24]

Montesquieu and Tocqueville believed that the State and political life in general tended to try to crush one of its most vital prerequisites (a rich associational life) and to seek to establish itself as the only necessary community.[25] This is, in many respects, what occurred in France. The Bourbon monarchy engaged in a process of slowly diluting the power of local intermediate groups such as the *parlements*. Hence, as de Tocqueville noted, "When the love of the French for political liberty reawakened, they had already formed certain notions concerning government that were not merely out of harmony with the existence of free institutions. They were all but contrary to them."[26]

The Freedom of Commercial Order

Explaining the rise of what we call "civil society" resists reduction to one common denominator. Such is the power, however, of civil society's commercial dimension in the modern world, that we are bound to consider its implications for the pursuit of integral liberty.

Even among the earliest observers of the spread of commerce, we can discern concerns about its implications for freedom. Ferguson expressed distinct anxieties about the effects of mounting material progress upon what he called "civic virtue." To an extent, Ferguson was simply echoing Aristotle's negative view of commerce. Profit did not, in Aristotle's view, contribute to human flourishing. Hence, pursuit of profit for its own sake was a disreputable form of behavior.[27]

Whatever one thinks of Aristotle's position, the market unquestionably provides people with powerful incentives to act in particular ways. But does it necessarily lead to a diminution of the conditions that encourage human flourishing?

On one level, commercial society has contributed to a healthy limiting of the State's ability to unreasonably obstruct our capacity to make free choices. Aquinas once wrote that the power of households to manage their own economic affairs—a power that depends on the assurance associated with property ownership—is the foundation of their ability to tell the State's rulers that their powers are limited. It is surely not coincidental that where commercial societies emerged, the capacity of State institutions to behave tyrannically became more limited. One need only compare the respective political development of Western, Central, and Eastern Europe. While all their societies dabbled in absolutism at different stages, it lasted the longest in those societies where private commercial activity was limited.[28]

One ought, of course, to hesitate before drawing too many conclusions from such comparisons. *"Laissez faire, laissez passer"* was the motto of Jacques Turgot and the eighteenth-century Physiocrats who sought to free economic life from tariffs and protectionist barriers. Yet, as Guizot once remarked, while "M. Turgot professed it more than anyone . . . in his brief administration, he was the minister who handed down the greatest number of rulings and ministerial orders, was in touch with the greatest number of interests, and made the most frequent use of authority."[29]

Still, through its attention to the power of choice, a commercial order has great potential to assist people's pursuit of integral fulfillment. The free economy is, after all, incomprehensible without its emphasis upon individual choice in the production and purchase of material goods and services. In market-influenced societies, people are encouraged to be independent and make choices, especially by the medium of contract. Contracts make many relationships necessarily conditional upon the individual wills that bring them into being. Though contracts, we make ourselves the author of particular obligations and limit our own capacity for acting by whim.

This reality is sometimes obscured by a tendency to speak of the "market" as if it were an anonymous conglomerate that exerts its own will. Certainly there is an "abstract" dimension to market economies in the sense that they are premised, as the German economists of the twentieth-century *ordo liberal* school stressed,[30] upon widespread acceptance of certain rules and institutions. These rules include the law of contract, while the institutions are exemplified by private property. These, in turn, presuppose the existence of public order guaranteed by State authority, not simply because contracts would otherwise be unenforceable, but because no individual would be willing to commit himself to a contract.[31]

Yet, while they are essential, these rules and institutions remain ancillary to what is truly central to market exchanges: human persons, human choices, and human acts. As observed by the Italian philosopher Rocco Buttiglione:

> The smallest element of the free market is a contract, the encounter of the free will of two human beings. They must both be free, for if they are not there can be no contract, and thus no free market. In this way, the law on contracts that stands at the very basis of a free-market economy is a law that presupposes human freedom.[32]

Note that Buttiglione does not justify the market on the empirical basis that it is the most efficient system for allocating scarce resources. Rather, he emphasizes that it is a moral requirement of a social order that takes the idea of freedom seriously by allowing people to assume responsibility for themselves in the economic sphere. Similar arguments are found in the writings of the quintessential *ordo liberal* scholar, Wilhelm Röpke. History illustrated, he insisted, that only a market economic order had proved able to give individuals the necessary scope for free choice in the material realm. Hence, we should not be surprised to see Röpke explaining in 1953 that "my opposition on technical grounds is that socialism, in its enthusiasm for organization, centralization, and efficiency, is committed to means that simply are not compatible with freedom."[33] "My fundamental opposition to socialism," Röpke wrote, "is to an ideology that, in spite of all its 'liberal' phraseology, gives too little to man, his freedom, and his personality; and too much to society."[34]

The force of Röpke's point become more apparent when we remember that State power was most frequently employed in the economic realm in the twentieth century as part of an effort to reduce material inequalities and diminish poverty. It does seem that this development had profound implications for many people's ability to achieve integral liberty. State-engineered redistributions of wealth do result in some people acquiring access to material things that they might not have otherwise gained. In some cases, this may increase their ability to pursue integral liberty insofar as it gives people things that assist them to acquire various basic goods.

The same forms of State interventionism can, however, seriously damage a society's moral ecology. In an 1835 article, de Tocqueville observed that while the poor law helped those in need, it failed to distinguish between the indigent and the lazy. Moreover, it resulted in a system in which the wealthy were required to pay money for the upkeep of payments that were a source of embarrassment for many of those in need. It was therefore, in de Tocqueville's view, both financially and morally destructive.[35]

By "moral destruction," de Tocqueville had in mind a breakdown of the moral sympathies that bind people together. Perhaps even more damaging is the manner in which such intervention can create disincentives for people to act directly for one or more of the basic goods.

When assistance to those in need is directly implemented through the political community, it reduces the incentives for individuals, families, and intermediate associations to choose directly the good of others. This State welfarism may even undermine the ability of such individuals and groups to act for the good of others by taking away some of the material resources that they require to do so. Expansive welfare States also diminish our opportunities to engage in practical reasoning by empowering State organs to make most decisions about how to help the poor. Few, moreover, would dispute that expansive welfare programs diminish the incentives for people to choose to work, and thereby participate in the basic good of skillful performance. From this standpoint, the natural law scholar Joseph Boyle suggests that "there is a significant limit on the extent to which the polity can provide welfare rights."[36]

The Limits of Markets

Neither Buttiglione nor Röpke believe that the market is in itself sufficient for creating conditions that facilitate integral liberty. Both understand that no set of economic arrangements makes sense until it is grounded in a moral and political theory that identifies the social arrangements that the economy is supposed to serve. No doubt, Buttiglione and Röpke are also aware that all economic theories—whether Marxist or liberal, indeed, even uniquely monetary ones—are based on implicit anthropological presumptions. The capacity of commercial life to contribute to a society in which integral liberty is easier to attain depends very much upon the vision of the person that underlies economic activity.

Most economic theory generally operates upon the anthropological assumption of man as *homo economicus:* the human person as the ultimate pleasure calculator. This creature seeks only to maximize personal satisfaction. His actions are focused on the calculation of costs and benefits from a narrowly self-interested standpoint. The same creature will evade rules if he can and will tend to keep them only if he believes that it is in his material self-interest to do so. In short, *homo economicus* is somewhat of a sociopath to whom the idea of integral liberty is, at best, a convenient rationalization.[37]

While few economists suggest that this model captures the complexity of human beings, it is not a neutral model. The philosophical viewpoint most akin to it is essentially a crude form of utilitarianism: That which is "good" is what provides most people with pleasure, satisfaction, and utility, and each person's idea of what is pleasurable is purely a matter of subjective preference.

Curiously such an anthropology of man is as almost as reductionist as that promoted by Marxism, an ideology that, broadly speaking, holds that *every* idea, institution, and event simply manifests the ongoing class struggle for control of the means of production. It was, after all, Marx who claimed that everything is essentially an ideological superstructure reflecting economic relationships.

Much economic anthropology is thus an inadequate grounding for a commercial order that contributes to conditions that facilitate human fulfillment. Even in themselves, commercial orders can diminish these conditions. One result of the multiplication of wants generated by a market economy is greater economic growth, but also much disappointment. Market orders imply that a large number of businesses will not be successful. This inevitability exacts a price in terms of people's morale.

Then there are the potentially negative effects of commercial life upon a society's moral ecology. The obvious risk is that wealth-creation may come to be viewed as an end in itself. In a reasoned concept of liberty, wealth is only instrumental to the fulfillment of persons. In itself, wealth does not represent the actualization of any intrinsic goods. Even if one views the economic process as a complex process of production, distribution, and consumption, wealth remains instrumental.

The question may, however, be asked: If the market economic order reflects, in part, the workings of each individual's self-interest, does this not implicitly undermine our capacity to pursue particular basic goods, such as friendship, that are at the core of integral liberty? Does it not distract us from establishing conditions that help others to fulfill themselves?

The answer is yes and no. The nature of market competition is such that it cannot be expected to mirror the life of a community of monks. To this extent, commercial relations tend not to embrace the degree of self-giving that occurs, for example, in family life. Reason, however, also tells us that different forms of communities have naturally different purposes. We should not therefore expect them all to be groups like the family or the nation-state. Here it is useful to pay heed to John Finnis's useful distinctions between a variety of relationships such as "business," "play," and "friendship," all of which are embodied, to varying degrees, in any form of community.[38] The different relative strengths of these relationships within any one community make all associations naturally conducive to certain activities and less conducive to others. The good of marriage, for example, is the participation of a man and a woman in the same good of an exclusive and life-long self-giving to each other that is consummated through sexual acts of the reproductive type. The same cannot be said of a business relationship in which two or more people may cooperate in order to participate individually in different goods.

At the same time, market economies do promote many material and social developments that contribute to the common good. Leaving aside their effective provision of the material basis required by any group of humans for existence, individuals are able to serve each other, albeit often indirectly, in commercial societies through the process of exchange. The market also brings people from very different backgrounds into contact with one another, while simultaneously reducing the potential for conflict by softening the intensity of political life. Echoing earlier reflections of Montesquieu on the effects of commercial life, de Tocqueville claimed:

> Trade is the natural enemy of all violent passions. Trade loves moderation, delights in compromise, and is most careful to avoid anger. It is patient, supple, and insinuating, only resorting to extreme means in cases of absolute necessity. Trade makes men independent of one another ... it leads them to want to manage their own affairs and teaches them how to succeed therein. Hence, it makes them inclined to liberty but disinclined to revolution.[39]

Tocqueville was not, however, naïve. In *Democracy in America*, he noted that the commercial republicanism generated by the market carried a risk of excessive regard for material goods.

Nor, however, should we underestimate the extent to which commerce can also be conducive to participation in basic goods such as practical reasonableness, skillful performance, and friendship.[40] Careful reflection upon the nature of contracts underlines this point.[41] When people make a contract, they are engaging in a commercial convention and a recognized legal practice. Such an activity presupposes a basic exercise in promise making in which we make a reasoned choice to commit ourselves to performing certain actions. Contracts are, in fact, null and void without such prior commitments. They therefore enlist our willingness to be truthful and act upon reasonable promises and commitments made. In this sense, they require us to act in a practically reasonable manner. To this extent, the very act of entering into a contract can directly facilitate human flourishing.

Echoes of the Transcendent

None of this attention to commerce's capacity to enhance the conditions required for integral liberty should distract us from the particular challenges generated by market orders, but nor should we overestimate the ability of market exchange to divert us from the pursuit of integral liberty. Such distractions may also be found in a variety of nonmarket contexts. Certainly we may seek to participate in basic goods in a commercial context and strive to resist the temptation of regarding wealth as a basic good. We may, however, also encounter analogous enticements in other forms of associational life. Even at the political level, the task of acquiring integral liberty requires us to struggle against the destiny of soft despotism potentially associated with democracy

Given the number, range, and depth of internal and external impediments to our achievement of integral liberty, the task of establishing a political and social order that encourages us to pursue such an end seems extremely difficult.

Ultimately, the case for ordered freedom continues to rest on its ability to meet the requirements of right reason, and the inability of the various utilitarian, consequentialist, and emotivist alternatives to do so. Who, however, does not wonder at the persistence and popularity of such ways of thinking, despite their demonstrated erroneousness?

Part of the answer may lie in the fact that even if we accept the truth of the basic goods and their centrality to integral liberty, human reason also tells us that our ability to participate in the basic goods is limited. Our capacity to engage in skillful performance begins to disintegrate. Our husbands and wives die. Even the capacity of many to act in accordance with practical reason becomes ravaged by disease and old age. All of us are ultimately confronted with the impasse of individual extinction, which renders impossible any further flourishing and scatters whatever has been accomplished into dust.

Or does it? Who does not wonder whether reason itself and our potential for integral liberty points to a reality that simultaneously encompasses and transcends the requirements of practical reason, a reality that brings illumination to the fragments of our lives? Certainly our free choices may contribute to the establishment of conditions that assist others to achieve self-mastery, but is it possible to make any further sense of this journey? Does man's finite liberty, in fact, encounter the infinite liberty of the Divine that man can know but which he is incapable of postulating by himself?[42] And if we conclude that there is further meaning to human liberty—that its significance reaches beyond history to that which is outside time and change—what are the implications of this for how we should act in the conditions of modern, even postmodern, pluralism? Such questions inevitably move us toward reflecting upon the meaning of an act of religious faith for living in a free society.

Notes

1. See Pierre Manent, *Tocqueville and the Nature of Democracy* (Lanham, Md.: Rowman and Littlefield, 1996), ix.

2. Guizot, "Philosophie politique: de la souveraineté," 343.

3. Friedrich Hayek, *Law, Legislation, and Liberty*, vol. 3, *The Political Order of a Free People* (Chicago: University of Chicago Press, 1979), 5.

4. Hayek, *The Political Order of a Free People*, 5.

5. Berlin, "Two Concepts of Liberty," 234–37.

6. Tocqueville, *Democracy*, 527.

7. For elaboration of this point, see Manent, *Tocqueville and the Nature of Democracy*, 29–36.

8. Tocqueville, *Democracy*, 505.

9. Ibid., 173.

10. Ibid., 694.

11. Tocqueville, *Democracy*, 93.

12. See Pierre Manent, *Modern Liberty and Its Discontents*, ed. and trans. Daniel Mahoney and Paul Seaton (Lanham, Md.: Rowman and Littlefield, 1998), 122–31.

13. See *Debates in the Several State Conventions on the Adoption of the Federal Constitution* (20 June 1788, Virginia), ed. Jonathon Elliot (Philadelphia: Lippincott Press, 1907).

14. See Michael Novak, *On Cultivating Liberty: Reflections on Moral Ecology*, ed. Brian Anderson (Lanham: Rowman and Littlefield, 1999), 9–31.

15. See Benjamin Constant, *De la liberté des anciens comparée à celles des modernes* (Paris: Éditions d'Aujourdhui, 1948), 119.

16. Cited in Carol Blum, *Rousseau and the Republic of Virtue* (Ithaca, N.Y.: Cornell University Press, 1986), 111.

17. Bernard de Jouvenal, *On Power* (Indianapolis: Liberty Press, 1991), 244–53.

18. Cited in William Sewell, "Collective Violence and Collective Loyalties in France: Why the French Revolution Made a Difference," *Politics and Society*, 18, no. 4 (1990): 543.

19. Tocqueville, *Democracy*, 515.

20. See John Keane, "Despotism and Democracy: The Origins and Development of the Distinction Between Civil Society and the State 1750–1850," in *Civil Society and the State: New European Perspectives* (London: Verso, 1988), 36. See also Aristotle, *Politics*, I, 1252a, 6–7.

21. See Z. A. Pelczynski, "Introduction," in *The State and Civil Society: Studies of Hegel's Political Philosophy*, ed. Z. A. Pelczynski (Cambridge: Cambridge University Press, 1984), iv–ix.

22. Friedrich Engels, "Ludwig Feuerbach and the End of Classical German Philosophy," *Selected Works*, vol. 3 (London: Penguin, 1971), 369. See also Karl Marx and Friedrich Engels, *The German Ideology* in *Selected Works*, vol. 3 (London: Penguin, 1971), 36.

23. See Manent, *Modern Liberty*, 222–23.

24. Keane, "Despotism and Democracy," 65.

25. See Montesquieu, *The Spirit of the Laws*, bk. 3, chap. 2.

26. Tocqueville, *Democracy*, 216.

27. Aristotle, *Politics* (Cambridge: Cambridge University Press, 1988), I.3.1257b1–1258a18.

28. See Jenö Szücs, "Three Historical Regions of Europe," in *Civil Society and the State*, 333–60.

29. François Guizot, *Des moyens de gouvernement et d'opposition dan l'état actuel de la France* (Paris: Éditions d'Aujourdhui, 1965), 174.

30. See, for example, Walter Eucken, *Grundsätze der Wirtschaftspolitik* (Tübingen: Mohr Siebeck, 1952); Franz Böhm, "The Rule of Law in a Market Economy," in *Germany's Social Market Economy: Origins and Evolution*, ed. A. Peacock and H. Willgerodt (London: Macmillan, 1989), 115–31

31. See Scruton, *Meaning of Conservatism*, 30.

32. Rocco Buttiglione, *The Moral Mandate for Freedom: Reflections on "Centesimus Annus"* (Grand Rapids, Mich.: Acton Institute, 1997), 7.

33. Wilhelm Röpke, "The Economic Necessity of Freedom," *Modern Age*, 3 (Summer 1959): 230.

34. Ibid., 230.

35. See Alexis de Tocqueville, "Mémoire sur le paupérisme," *Bulletin des Sciences economiques et sociales du Comité des traveux historiques et scientifiques* (Paris: Gaillot, 1911), 17–37.

36. Joseph Boyle, "Fairness in Holdings: A Natural Law Account of Property and Welfare Rights," *Social Philosophy and Policy*, 18, no. 1 (2001) 218.

37. A lengthier and more adequate treatment of this matter may be found in Samuel Gregg and Ian Harper, *Economics and Ethics: The Quarrel and the Dialogue* (Sydney: Center for Independent Studies, 1999).

38. See Finnis, *Natural Law*, 134–60.

39. Tocqueville, *Democracy*, 637.

40. See Buttiglione, *The Moral Mandate for Freedom*, 10.

41. See Finnis, *Natural Law*, 298–308.

42. See Henri de Lubac, S.J., *Le mystère du surnaturel* (Paris: Aubier, 1965).

7

Reflections of a "Catholic Whig"

*There is hardly any human action, however, private it may be,
which does not result from some very general concept that men
have of God, of His relations with the human race, of the
nature of their soul, and of their duties to their fellows. Nothing
can prevent such ideas from being the common spring from
which all else originates.*

—Alexis de Tocqueville[1]

At first glance, it may seem odd to end this book with a chapter on the place of
religious believers in a free society. Why should those with religious convictions
be given any special consideration? Why should we not instead consider the situation of those in free societies who adopt explicitly antidemocratic political
commitments, or who hold an anarchic view of the social order?

Part of the answer lies in the fact that many liberal scholars have considered
some of these issues precisely by reflecting upon how religiously motivated
actions should be treated in free societies. In discussing the controversial matter
of abortion, both John Rawls and the philosopher Judith Jarvis Thomson single
out "Catholics" as one group whose purported arguments concerning the role of
law regarding this subject are, in their view, unreasonable in light of rational
reflection about how a society copes with the fact of difference.[2] Whatever one
thinks of their conclusions, Rawls and Thomson recognize that the existence of
people whose religious beliefs inform their actions in the public square raises

important questions about how modern liberal societies justly accommodate those who harbor doubts about aspects of secular liberalism.

Another reason for examining this subject is that many religious believers are themselves uncertain about the matter. A Catholic may, for instance, firmly believe that the Roman Catholic Church's teaching on matters of faith and morals is true. The same Catholic, however, may purport to be unclear about what this means for their participation in liberal democratic life. Are Catholics simply to pretend that modernity never happened? Or do they resolve that the political world is something cut off from the claims of God's kingdom? In short, do they regard their act of faith as a Catholic to be irrelevant when it comes to public life? Is justice indeed to be divorced from the good?

The "Catholic problem" is, then, a fruitful way of exploring the place of the religious believer—and, in a more general sense, the "nonliberal"—in modern liberal settings. The relevance of this chapter is thus not confined to Catholics but to anyone who questions the ability of liberal theories to be just toward those who have reservations about much contemporary liberal thinking about the free society.

Liberal, Conservative, Tory, Whig?

When defining their political position, many Catholics label themselves by attaching a political term to their Catholic identity. Hence, we see expressions such as "Catholic conservative," "Catholic liberal," or "Catholic neoconservative" appear regularly. A less frequently used phrase is "Catholic Whig." This term is found in the writings of the theologian Michael Novak, who employs it to convey the precise nature of his political identity and inspiration.[3] Taken from the name of the political party that slowly reduced the power of the British monarchy in the seventeenth and eighteenth centuries, the word "Whig" is used in this context to describe a commitment to the genuine achievement represented by the emergence of constitutionalism, limited government, rule of law, a flourishing set of civil associations, and a free economy in the "Anglo-Saxon" world. It also has the advantage of allowing Novak to avoid utilizing those highly ambiguous phrases "conservative" and "liberal" (though one sometimes wonders if "Whig" is any less indefinite or, indeed, rather problematic given the morally dubious political machinations pursued by particular seventeenth-century Whig figures such as the Earl of Shaftsbury).[4] *Catholic* Whig additionally permits Novak to delineate clearly his ambition: to produce a synthesis of the institutions that many secular liberals have long claimed as their own, with the philosophy of man expressed in the visions of ancients such as Aristotle but decisively modified by Catholicism, especially through Aquinas.

We may, of course, ask if it is appropriate to attach the name of one's faith commitment to any political label, be it liberal, Marxist, or Fascist. For if someone believes that the Catholic Church teaches the truth about God and man, then using the term "Catholic" as an adjective may suggest that he treats that faith as simply one of many influences upon his political identity, rather than regarding the Catholic faith as central to his life, including his political commitments. What should matter for a Catholic is not whether a position is "Tory," "anarchist," or "Whig." *What matters is whether a political stance meets the demands of right reason.*

In spite of these limitations, the phrase Catholic Whig may prove useful for some Catholics seeking to give a more precise definition to their relationship as Catholics with the modern world as well as the view that they take of secular liberal modernity. The importance of this lies in the fact that, in many respects, the determination of a coherent stance vis-à-vis the modern world has proved to be a source of considerable trauma for Catholics since the eighteenth century.

A Catholic in the World

For the Christian, "the world" has a number of different connotations. In Scripture, the world is often presented as something different from Christ's kingdom (John 18:37). At other times, the world is seen as the sphere in which salvation occurs. Then again, "the ruler of the world" is clearly Satan. Evil is real and regarded as present in "the world." The very word *church* in the original Greek (*ekklesia*) means "called out." The Church thus consists of those people whom God has called out of the world.

The world thus has neutral, positive, and negative connotations. For the Catholic, the point is that *all* of these are true. All three pictures are woven into Catholic belief, and the complexity of this is easily ignored in favor of one image.

A common mistake is to reduce the kingdom of God to the pursuit of justice in this world. The often unspoken assumption underlying such views is that the kingdom of God and its divine justice can become terrestrial realties on a human scale. Scripture itself warns believers against the tendency to reduce God to an element of the created world. The point is put more polemically by the Italian theologian, Alessandro Maggiolini:

> To resolve the problems of poverty and social justice, I don't think that it was necessary for the Word to be made flesh, die on the Cross, and be resurrected for us and our salvation. The wisdom of some political sage or the impetus of some revolutionaries would have been sufficient.[5]

Certainly, if the disorder that Catholics call "sin" was not in the world, we might be able to imagine a utopia where humans would have no need for a Saviour. The Church has always, however, taught that because man is wounded by sin, heaven-on-earth is impossible. Present arrangements, from a Catholic perspective, are always only tentative. They will be subsumed into a total redeemed world only when Christ returns.

Too, if uncritical engagement with the world is not an alternative for Catholics faithful to the Church's teaching, nor is the approach of a fortress Church that disdains the world. Such a position usually implies viewing the world, especially the modern world, as irredeemably hostile to the Catholic faith.

Though mistaken, the temptation to embrace such ideas is comprehensible. Modernity's emphasis upon progress (however vaguely defined) has encouraged some Catholics to think that because the Church advocates certain unchangeable truths, they are "behind the times" or "not progressive." In more than one instance, Catholics have allowed their apostolic, pastoral, and spiritual activities to become fixated with temporal fashions and transitory tendencies. Some have forgotten the Second Vatican Council's affirmation "that underlying all that changes there are many things that do not change, and that have their ultimate foundation in Christ who is the same yesterday, today, and forever."[6] To forget this and to allow the Church to become a mere appendage to secular political agendas—be they Marxist, feminist, homosexual, or even conservative in nature—is the surest way to trivialize the Gospel and reduce Catholics to being what Lenin once famously described as "useful idiots."

But the ongoing problem of some Catholics' uncritical acceptance of the world does not legitimate withdrawal from the world. The Catholic life is not limited to the proper ordering of personal moral life. It also has a social dimension, not least because social life presents man with dilemmas to which Catholics must respond by acting in ways that, like all freely chosen acts, meet the demands of truth. Though Catholics cannot and should not equate their ultimate salvation with the establishment of a more humane temporal order, bringing the love and truth of the Gospel to the world means that they cannot ignore the world, however disordered it may be.

A possible alternative for Catholics who recognize the unreasonableness of both uncritical assimilation and total withdrawal is that of the "Catholic Whig." Apart from expressing a Catholic's genuine commitment to "Whig" institutions such as constitutionalism and rule of law, the phrase also denotes the same person's unambiguous commitment to what the Catholic Church has always taught on matters on faith and morals to be true. We also use "Catholic" here to state that there are *universal* basic goods that can be known and accessed by all who possess unimpaired reason. Finally, "Catholic" is additionally employed to indicate openness to the discovery of insights into the truth made outside the Church. This has always been intrinsic to the Catholic tradition, as evidenced by Saint Paul's appeal to Stoic philosophers in the Areopagus, Augustine's use of Platonic thought, and Aquinas's assimilation of Aristotle.

The Catholic Whig position is thus to state that the kingdom of God is not of this world. It belongs to a different order: that of revelation and fidelity to God. The Reign of God does belong, after all, to God rather than to man. This, however, is perfectly compatible with stating that the transcendent does and must shed light on everything, though it cannot be reduced to any temporal activity in which humans are engaged. Hence, Catholics must work to help the world—and

Whig institutions—become more firmly grounded in what Revelation and practical reason tells us is good and true, without imagining that either humans or Whig institutions can achieve justice in the world in the divine sense of the word.

In the midst of this critical engagement with the world, perhaps the greatest temptation for Catholic Whigs is to become selective with regard to the principles of their Catholic faith in order to smooth over inevitable conflicts with aspects of secular modernity. An associated challenge is to remember that it is the prerogative of the Church—not other parts of society or the media—to decide whether a particular concept or expression is part of the Catholic faith. Moreover, Catholics should avoid simply identifying the opinion of other Catholics (many of whom have more or less completely conformed to the surrounding secular culture in which they live) or an apparent consensus of "contemporary theologians" purely and simply as what is known as the *sensus fidei* (the idea that through the Holy Spirit of Truth, Christ has given the whole body of believers a supernatural and infallible instinct for what is orthodox faith). This phrase, from the Catholic standpoint, implies by its very nature a profound agreement of mind and heart *with* the Church (*sentire cum Ecclesia*), which is a communion of the living *and* the dead. Though theological faith cannot err, believers can still hold erroneous views because not all their thoughts spring from the Catholic faith.[7] Not all the ideas circulating among Catholics are compatible with the Catholic faith.

Yet precisely because the Catholic Whig *is* committed to an engagement with secular modernity, he must find a way to engage the world in terms that it can understand. By this, we do not imply a mere transposing of Christian truth into the terminology of a particular ideology. In all such cases, Christian truth is eventually subordinated to the ideology's needs. Rather, we mean the articulation of comprehensive reasons concerning the truth about man and its implications for the social order.

Catholic scholars have never shied away from arguing a case based on reason. Aquinas was once asked: Should one settle disputed questions by reason or by authority? His response, though lengthy, remains as relevant now as it was then:

> Any activity is to be pursued in a way appropriate to its purpose. Disputations have one or other of two purposes.
>
> One is designed to remove doubts about whether such-and-such is so. In disputations of this sort you should above all use authorities acceptable to those with whom you are disputing; with Jews, for example, you should appeal to the authority of the Old Testament; with Manichees, who reject the Old Testament, you should use only the New; with Christians who have split off from us, for example, the Greeks [Orthodox], who accept both Testaments but reject the teaching of our [Catholic] Saints, you should rely on the authority of the Old and New Testaments and those of the Church teachers they do accept. And if you are disputing with people who accept no authority, you must resort to natural reasons.

Then there is the professorial academic disputation, designed not for removing error but for teaching, so that those listening may be led to an understanding of the truth with which the professor is concerned. And here you must rely upon reasons, reasons that track down the root of the truth and create a real knowledge of how it is that your assertions are true. Otherwise, if professors settle questions by bare authorities, listeners are indeed told that such-and-such is so but gain nothing in the way of knowledge or understanding and go away empty.[8]

Confronting Secularist Intolerance

Such is the approach and inspiration that underlines the Catholic Whig idea. There are, however, serious questions as to whether the modern liberal polity will allow Catholics to engage the world in these terms. There is much to suggest that liberal secularism expects Catholics wishing to participate in the public square to essentially renounce the content of their identity as Catholics and become, for all intents and purposes, liberal secularists.

The wariness with which many of a secularist mindset have viewed Catholics and the Catholic Church emerged in the wake of the French Revolution and was reflected in the antireligious impulse that quickly established itself as a revolutionary (and later continental liberal) orthodoxy. As a Catholic (albeit one who struggled with the act of faith) and a political thinker who wished to heal the breach between the Church and the post-Revolutionary political order, de Tocqueville was acutely conscious of this. "One of the first steps of the French Revolution," he wrote, "had been to attack the Church, and, among the passions that were born of the Revolution, the first to be kindled and the last to be extinguished was the passion of irreligion."[9] This had little to do with the ongoing phenomenon of anticlericalism. Rather, it owed much to a sense that religion, especially Catholicism, was the height of superstition and thus, an obstacle to progress. The archetypal expression of this sentiment can be found in a recorded remark of Georges-Jacques Danton, a key figure into pushing the Revolution toward terrorist policies that eventually resulted in Danton himself losing his head: "These priests, this nobility are not guilty, but they have to die, because they are out of place, they hinder the movement of things and get in the way of the future."[10]

Writing from Königsberg in the same century that Danton and other Jacobins were engaged in such violence against the Church in the name of progress, Immanuel Kant identified the intellectual and moral problems with such appeals to the demands of "progress," in which the basic point of good actions is considered to involve their contribution to some future good condition of the future human race.

What remains disconcerting about all this is firstly, that the earlier generations seem to perform their laborious tasks only for the sake of the later ones, so as to prepare for them a further stage from which they can raise still higher the structure intended by nature; and secondly, that only the later generations will in fact have the good fortune to inhabit the building on which a whole series of their forefathers (admittedly, without any conscious intention) had worked without themselves being able to share in the happiness they were preparing.[11]

From this standpoint, appeals to progress can be used to justify the most horrendous acts, ranging from the establishing of a Marxist proletariat dictatorship in order to "speed up" history, to the practice of conducting medical experiments that destroy human life in order to discover new ways of saving or enhancing human life. In less dramatic terms, the same appeal may lead, as Roger Scruton stresses, to a profusion throughout the public square of a sense that anything can and should be altered,[12] with the possibility of change being the only necessary justification. It also facilitates one of the more dangerous secular myths: that things "go forward" since that is their nature. History and political life are thus spoken of in terms of movement forward or backward. Hence, the "liberal" advances progress, while the "conservative" impedes it.[13] "Good" becomes understood as change, while "evil" is resistance to change, no matter what its content.

Though the fierceness of some secularists' commitments to "progress" never managed to obliterate religion, it has created new challenges for Catholics to address. In attempting to break the Church's authority (as an apparent obstacle to "progress"), many secularists found themselves having to deny the validity of thinking about freedom in terms of its ultimate end, that is, salvation. Freed from this authority, secular modernity tends to conceptualize freedom as liberation of the will, whereby man's will is "liberated" from the distinctly human goods discernable by practical reason. In thus liberating his will, man risks undermining his very humanity itself.

We know, moreover, that those claiming to be free from moral absolutes find it difficult to let their commitment to relativity remain relative. They invariably seek to make it an absolute. Even atheism carries the indelible mark of faith, precisely because it can only define itself in opposition to religious belief. As one of the characters in Fyodor Dostoevsky's *The Brothers Karamazow* says, "to live without God is nothing but torture . . . Man cannot live without kneeling. He could not bear it, nobody would be capable of it; if he rejects God, he kneels before an idol of wood or gold, or an imaginary one. They are all idolaters and not atheists."[14] Perhaps from observing the aggressive anti-Catholicism of many nineteenth-century French liberals, de Tocqueville arrived at the same conclusion.

In ages of fervor, it sometimes happens that men abandon their religion, but they only escape from its yoke in order to submit to that of another. Faith changes its allegiance but does not die. Then the former religion arouses in all hearts ardent love or implacable hatred; some leave it in anger, others cling to it with renewed ardor: Beliefs differ, but irreligion is unknown.[15]

To their credit, many liberals acknowledge some of the genuine difficulties that liberal modernity continues to pose for Catholics. In a famous essay in which he distinguished "liberalism" from "conservatism," Hayek (a professed agnostic) insisted:

Unlike the rationalism of the French Revolution, true liberalism has no quarrel with religion, and I can only deplore the militant and essentially illiberal anti-religionism which animated so much of nineteenth-century Continental liberalism. . . . What distinguishes the liberal from the conservative is that, however profound his own spiritual beliefs, he will never regard himself as entitled to impose them on others and that for him the spiritual and the temporal are different spheres which ought not to be confused.[16]

Hayek certainly recognizes the inherent contradiction of the antireligious spirit that has animated many liberals insofar as it leads them to promote policies that are highly intolerant of religious believers. Yet, the view of religion taken by even this most sympathetic of liberals itself has the potential to create dilemmas for Catholics.

If Hayek is simply suggesting that people should not seek to impose their religious beliefs on others, especially through the force of law, then Catholics can express sympathy with his position. To believe, truly means choosing freely. Christianity has always affirmed, as the Second Vatican Council II stressed, that it is wrong to try to force others to become Christians,[17] even though this maxim has been ignored by some Christians in the past.

At another level, however, much depends upon what Hayek means by "the spiritual" and "the temporal." If he means that the spiritual is the world of Revelation and the temporal is the world of reason, then Catholics see no conflict between the two. Faith and reason, in the Catholic faith, complement and assist each other. The truth known through faith does not contradict the truth known through reason.

For Catholics, the spiritual and the temporal are indeed different but also part of the same reality. A difficulty thus emerges if this difference, in Hayek's view, requires separation of the spiritual and the temporal. For he would be effectively asking Catholics to deny the essence of what they believe humans to be: spiritual and material beings whose ultimate destiny is either heaven or hell, a destiny that depends partly upon their free choices in this life, including those choices that occur in the public square. The demands of the transcendental have profound implications for a faithful Catholic's actions in the temporal world.

They must therefore hope that Hayek is not implying that Catholics living in liberal polities should adopt civic characters as ahistorical beings and who focus on procedural matters rather than discerning what are reasonable and good choices for the life of a political community.

One way that various Catholics have sought to overcome some of the problems above has been to avoid appeals to religious authorities such as Scripture, Tradition, and Magisterium when contributing to debates in the public square. In this regard, various Catholic scholars have expressed some sympathy with John Rawls' position that debates in the public square in pluralist societies ought to be based on appeals to public reason. The difficulty, as many Catholic and liberal scholars have observed, is the sheer "thinness" of the definition of public reason offered by Rawls (which assumes that all desires are prima facie entitled to satisfaction),[18] not to mention his problematic separation of reason and truth.

Some liberals have recognized these Catholic concerns about liberal modernity as genuine problems. William Galston speaks rather bravely, for example, about the dangers of "exclusionary liberalism" or "liberal imperialism."[19] He also suggests that his fellow liberals need to reconsider the idea of "value pluralism" and disassociate it from any notion of relativistic leveling. This is important, in Galston's view, because "the distinction between good and evil is real and inscribed in the nature of things."[20]

Yet, in the very same article in which he makes these suggestions, Galston arrives at conclusions that sound remarkably Rawlsian in character, and raise doubts about his willingness to accord Catholics an equal place in the public square. According to Galston:

> Liberals for their part must reject the use of theology and natural law as a basis for coercive State policy. It is one thing for Catholics, reasoning within the premises of their community, to reach conclusions about abortion, assisted suicide, and homosexuality that are held to be binding on the faithful; quite another to impose those views on others. Catholics may be affronted by a legal code that permits acts they view as abominable. But in circumstances of deep moral diversity, the alternative to enduring these affronts is even worse.[21]

Some peculiar assumptions underlie these words. First, Galston seems to presume that natural law is a specifically Catholic way of moral reasoning. By definition, *this is simply not true*. The "father" of natural law, Aristotle, was a pagan. Jewish, Protestant, and secular thinkers have also ascribed to the notion that practical reason can allow us to know certain moral truths, regardless of the community or religious tradition to which people happen to belong.[22]

Second, Galston appears unaware that while there are many teachings of the Catholic faith that are not fully comprehensible to natural reason (such as the doctrine of the Trinity), there are also many teachings (such as the existence of God and that killing innocent human life is always wrong) that *are* accessible to practical reason unaided by Revelation (Aquinas called these the "preambles to faith"). For issues such as abortion, euthanasia, and homosexual "marriage" are not "Catholic" issues. While many Catholics may be prominent opponents of the legalization of such activities, their arguments can be presented in terms of public reason without any appeal to Catholic faith or Revelation.[23]

Here, some Catholics would do well to recall that the fact of man's ability to access various truths by reason is considered to be a matter of Catholic faith and was defined as such by the First Vatican Council: "If anyone says the one true God, our Creator and Lord, cannot be known with certainty by the natural light of human reason through the things that are created: *anathema sit*."[24] This clearly refutes the common assumption outside (and often inside) the Catholic Church that anything that the Church proposes for acceptance is, by definition, a religious claim (religious belief being misrepresented incompatible with reason) and therefore indefensible in terms of reason.

Between Two Worlds

For all the past and present conflicts between Catholics and secularism, we should note that many liberals have affirmed that religion has a vital role to play in civilizing society. In de Tocqueville's mind, it was the nature of religious belief to influence human choices, thereby sustaining habits of action that he called *mœurs*. In articulating this position, de Tocqueville was driven by a particular concern:

> When a people's religion is destroyed, doubt invades the highest faculties of the mind and half paralyzes all the rest. Each man gets into the way of having nothing but confused and changing notions about the matters of greatest importance to himself and his fellows. Opinions are ill-defended or abandoned, and in despair of solving unaided the greatest problems of human destiny, men ignobly give up thinking about them. Such a state inevitably enervates the soul, and relaxing the springs of the will, prepares a people for bondage.[25]

Yet, for all Tocqueville's conviction that religion has beneficial effects upon a society, he is conspicuously silent about the truth-claims that are at the heart of religious belief. For de Tocqueville, religion meets various social needs in a democracy. He does not, however, view Catholicism or, for that matter, any other religion as providing the true account of reality. Tocqueville usually spoke about religion in terms of its social utility rather than its claim to embody and teach universal truths. "Society has nothing to fear or hope from an afterlife," he wrote, "and what is most important is not so much that all citizens profess the true religion but that they profess a religion."[26]

Such reasoning fails to recognize that those who are religious believers do *not* commonly understand their faith in this way. There may even be times when the truths of the Catholic faith require Catholics to challenge rather than affirm the dominant mores of a given society, regardless of the "disutility" of such actions. Indeed, the more religion is perceived in utility terms, the less "useful" it will become, for unless people are convinced of the *truth* of what they believe, the less they will be inclined to see infractions of the moral precepts proposed by their religious faith (and practical reason) as being important, and the less that religion will be able to contribute to maintaining the habits of action required by a free social order.

The fact, however, that some liberals think that religion can assist in preserving a free society should encourage Catholics to give even deeper thought to what they can intellectually contribute to such societies. Perhaps the most significant contribution is for Catholics to remind the world that freedom is something greater than free will. This is not to deny that a society of liberty necessarily contains much indeterminacy. The ability to choose demands much space, and is therefore inevitably associated with a certain degree of unpredictability. This alone suggests that Catholics should not seek to turn the free society into a "total society."

At the same time, Catholics should also intellectually oppose those who, wittingly or otherwise, seek to build a world in which choice in itself is considered the primary reference point for assessing an action's validity. Instead, Catholics should point to the integral liberty that comes from (1) recognizing the basic goods that lie at the heart of our humanity, and (2) choosing to live in that truth. It is, in fact, the responsibility of Catholics to speak of the Pauline liberty of the children of God: To explain that while free will is important, it is not enough if one wants to live an authentically human life.

True love for others does not involve obscuring the truth, especially moral truth, from them, for love without truth is sentimentalism. Thanks to truth, we can have a serious conversation about how life may be lived in a better, more human way. It also gives rise to the possibility of stating that certain things ought never be done, and a willingness to identify and confront untruth, including occasionally through law and legal prohibitions. Catholics must therefore resist the temptation to banish questions of morality to the private realm, as something so personal that no one dare question the validity of anyone's choices. Instead, Catholics should continue to propose the truth about the good to all people living in free societies, so that their consciences will be informed before they make the choices that will either enhance or diminish their integral liberty. Moreover, there is always the possibility that in doing so, Catholics will indirectly help others to discover the God who, they believe, is the source of the good: To realize, in a paraphrase of the twentieth-century Swiss theologian Hans Urs von Balthasar, that while man is a limited being in a limited world, our reason is open to the unlimited of the transcendent.[27]

This idea of the transcendent has always aroused hope and fear among people as they ponder whether they have merited salvation. This, oddly enough, also manifests itself among convinced secularists. At the end of his *Memoirs*, the French liberal philosopher Raymond Aron wrote that, as a young man, he and his friends spoke of realizing their "secular salvation."[28] Aron then asked himself, somewhat nervously, whether he had achieved it. This is, as Pierre Manent remarks, a very human question. No one can avoid it. Facing the ultimate prospect of death, we recognize that we can never assume complete control of our life. Hence, we are always asking, Toward what is my life flowing? Does oblivion await me? Does it matter whether or not I have participated in or denied the goods basic to my humanity?

It is difficult to see how the conclusion that man is ultimately destined for dissolution can lead to anything except despair. This has troubling social implications, because a community marked by despair is a society slowly marching into the quicksand of a culture of death.

Catholicism is, however, capable of giving people sound reasons for hope and ultimate reasons to live a truly human life. Moreover, it *must* do so. This observation was at the heart of von Balthasar's insight when he wrote:

> The Christians of today, living in a night that is deeper than that of the later Middle Ages, are given the task of performing the act of affirming Being, unperturbed by the darkness and the distortion, in a way that is vicarious and representative: an act that is at first theological, but which contains within itself the whole dimension of the metaphysical act of the affirmation of Being. Those who are directed in this way to pray continually, to find God in all things and to glorify him are able to do so on particular grounds (that is, particular graces) which allow them to perform their "creaturely duty." ... But insofar as they are to shine like "the stars in the sky," they are also entrusted with the task of bringing light to those areas of Being which are in darkness so that its primal light may shine anew not only upon them but also upon the whole world; for it is only in this light that man can walk in accordance with what he is truly called to be.[29]

The carrying out of this "creaturely duty" does not mean indulging in futile attempts to create heaven-on-earth. Instead, Catholicism teaches that our human choices for the good contribute in a mysterious way to the building of that kingdom that will be fully realized when Christ returns. It also proclaims that this realm will be inhabited by all who proved themselves followers of Christ through their choices for the truth that is Christ. This view of the ultimate significance of free choice is at the heart of the Second Vatican Council's teaching about the nature of human action:

> For after we have obeyed the Lord, and in His Spirit nurtured on earth the goods of human dignity, brotherhood, and freedom, and indeed all the good fruits of our nature and enterprise, we will find them again, but freed of stain, burnished and transfigured. This will be so when Christ hands over to the Father a kingdom eternal and universal: "a kingdom of truth and life, of holiness and grace, of justice, love, and peace." On this earth that kingdom is already present in mystery. When the Lord returns, it will be brought into full flower.[30]

Ultimately, the effectiveness of Catholics in realizing these goods depends upon their willingness to be faithful to the received truth. This places Catholics at odds with much of the contemporary secular mindset. One need only consider the case of Sir Thomas More. Some historians have negatively judged the effectiveness of More's refusal to swear the Oath of Succession demanded from all subjects of Henry VIII of England as part of the king's attempt to legitimize his marriage to Ann Boleyn. After all, More's death did nothing to stop the Tudor monarch's pillaging of the monasteries or his subordination of the Church in England to State power. Nor, in the longer term, did it stem what More may have foreseen as the effects of the turbulence produced by heresy—not just the violence perpetrated in the sixteenth and seventeenth centuries but the eventual rejection by much of Europe of Christ's divinity and finally the existence of God altogether.[31]

The Catholic does, however, have reason to hope that, whatever the efficacy of More's choice in this world, More's willingness to allow his finite liberty to be seized by love of God's infinite truth[32] contributed immeasurably to building up Christ's kingdom. For the Catholic, eternal life does not begin at the point of death. If it did, it would not be eternal. Instead, it is the one true life. Confronting the escape into an endless indulgence of passions offered by secular modernity or the flight into nothingness and self-annihilation presented by Asian mysticism, Catholicism upholds a liberty of love of the true and the good that integrates man as embodied intelligent freedom into the service of the coming kingdom of God,[33] the only place where human beings can find their own ultimate fulfillment.

The task of realizing the basic goods, however, need not always occur in a context of opposition to the temporal institutions in place. Catholics are certainly bound to oppose what the theologian Thomas Dubay describes as the dogmas of materialism: "the primacy of pleasure, the invalidity of metaphysics, . . . the relativity of morality . . . the denial of freedom."[34] Insofar as liberal modernity embraces these ideas or seeks to isolate man from all those unchosen aspects of himself that are, in fact, prerequisites to his freedom, Catholics must never hesitate to demonstrate their unreasonableness. The idea that man is nothing more than a conglomerate of passions and that human fulfillment consists of merely satisfying as many of those passions as possible in a short period of time, must be resisted and refuted over and over again. This need not, however, mean that those institutions commonly regarded as "liberal"—the market, the rule of law, a constitutionally limited State, a flourishing set of civil associations—should be considered inherently flawed by Catholics.

The liberalism that is wanting is a set of claims about the human person rather than its institutional associations. In part, this book has sought to show how such institutions can be grounded in a vision that avoids the common liberal reliance upon utilitarian assumptions. The task of achieving such a synthesis is nothing less than a civilizational mission that Catholics are in a unique position to foster.

By definition, this mission involves Catholics establishing themselves equidistant between those who hold that all was darkness before 1789, and those who believe that nothing but darkness has followed after 1789. The inability of some Catholics to do so has relegated them to the irrelevance of romantic nostalgia or the triviality of aping secular modernity. Until such tendencies are overcome, the ability of Catholics to contribute to the project of ordered liberty will continue to languish in the realm of possibility rather than of actuality. And this is important, for ultimately it is the free choices of many acting persons for this project that will bring about its realization rather than the decisions of governments.

We end, then, where we began: with Alexis de Tocqueville, a man of the old order who stood on the precipice of the modern world: A man who, despite his own struggle with Catholic faith, had no doubt that the emerging free societies of his time reflected the workings of Providence through the free actions of free men.

> Men think that the greatness of the idea of unity lies in means. God sees it in the end. It is for that reason that the idea of greatness leads to a thousand mean actions. To force all men to march in step toward the same goal—that is a human idea. To encourage endless variety of actions but to bring them about so that in a thousand different ways all tend toward the fulfillment of one great design—that is a God-given idea.
>
> The human idea of unity is almost always sterile, but that of God is immensely fruitful. Men think that they prove their greatness by simplifying the means. God's object is simple but His means infinitely various.[35]

Notes

1. Tocqueville, *Democracy*, 442–43.

2. See Rawls, *Political Liberalism*, 234–44, fn. 32; Judith Jarvis Thomson, "Abortion," *Boston Review*, 20 (1995): 15.

3. See Michael Novak, *The Catholic Ethic and the Spirit of Capitalism* (New York: Free Press, 1993), 167; Novak, *On Cultivating Liberty*, 145–90.

4. See, for example, John Kenyon, *The Popish Plot* (London: Heinemann, 1972).

5. Alessandro Maggiolini, "The End of Christianity As We Knew it?" *Inside the Vatican*, 9, no. 7 (2001): 75.

6. Second Vatican Council, Pastoral Constitution on the Church in the Modern World *Gaudium et Spes*, in A. Flannery, O.P., (gen. ed.), *Vatican Council II: The Conciliar and Post Conciliar Documents*, vol. 1 (rev. ed.) (Leominister: Fowler Wright Books Ltd., 1987), par. 10.

7. See Council of Trent, Session VI, c. 9, in Denzinger-Schonmetzer Collection of Church Documents in Jesuit Fathers of St. Mary's College, *The Church Teaches: Documents of the Church in English Translation* (Rockford: Tan Books and Publishers, 1973), no. 1534; and Aquinas, *ST*, q. 1, a. 3, ad. 3.

8. Thomas Aquinas, *Quaestiones de Quolibet Quodlibetal* IV, q. 9 a3c in *Thomae Aquinatis Opera Omnia cum Hypertextibus in CD-ROM.*

9. Alexis de Tocqueville, *L'Ancien Regime et la Révolution* (Paris: Gallimard, 1952), I, 83.

10. Quoted in François-René Chateaubriand, *Memoirs d'outre-tombe* (Paris: Flammarion, 1948), bk. 9, chap. 4.

11. Immanuel Kant, "Idea for a Universal History with a Cosmopolitan Purpose," in *Kant's Political Writings*, ed. Hans Reiss (Cambridge: Cambridge University Press, 1970), 44.

12. Scruton, *Meaning of Conservatism*, 22.

13. Ibid., 190–91.

14. Fyodor Dostoevsky, *The Brothers Karamazow* (London: Quartet, 1990), 271.

15. Tocqueville, *Democracy*, 299.

16. Hayek, *Constitution*, 407.

17. See Second Vatican Council, Declaration on Religious Liberty *Dignitatus Humanae*, in *Vatican Council II: The Conciliar and Post-Conciliar Documents*, vol. 1, par. 10.

18. See George, *The Clash of Orthodoxies*, 63–74.

19. William Galston, "Contending with Liberalism: Some Advice for Catholics," *Commonweal*, 128, no. 7 (2001): 14.

20. Galston, "Contending with Liberalism," 15.

21. Ibid.

22. See, for example, David Novak, *Natural Law in Judaism* (Cambridge: Cambridge University Press, 1998); J. Budziszewski, *Written on the Heart: The Case for Natural Law* (Chicago: Intervarsity Press, 1997).

23. See, for example, George, *The Clash of Orthodoxies*, 63–74.

24. Denzinger-Schonmetzer, no. 3026.

25. Tocqueville, *Democracy*, 444.

26. Ibid., 290.

27. Hans Urs von Balthasar, "A Resumé of My Thought," in *Hans Urs von Balthasar: His Life and Work*, ed. David Schindler (San Francisco: Communio Books/Ignatius Press, 1991), 1.

28. See Raymond Aron, *Mémoires* (Paris: Julliard, 1983), 772.

29. Hans Urs von Balthasar, *The Glory of the Lord: A Theological Aesthetics*, vol. 5, *The Realm of Metaphysics in the Modern Age* (Edinburgh: T. and T. Clark, 1991), 648–49.

30. Second Vatican Council, *Gaudium et Spes*, par. 39.

31. See James Monti, *The King's Good Servant but God's First: The Life and Writings of Saint Thomas More* (San Francisco: Ignatius Press, 1997), 453.

32. See Georges de Schrijver, *Le merveilleux accord de Dieu et de l'homme. Etude de l'analogie de l'être chez Hans Urs von Balthasar* (Leuven: BETL, 1983), 47.

33. See Marc Ouellet, "The Foundations of Christian Ethics," *Communio*, 17 (1990), 141.

34. Thomas Dubay, S.M., *Faith and Certitude* (San Francisco: Ignatius Press, 1985), 205.

35. Tocqueville, *Democracy*, 734–35.

INDEX

abortion, 51, 113, 114
absolutism, 76–77, 94, 97
action, human, 16, 18, 25, 37–45, 61, 85, 94, 116
Acton, Lord, xii, 2–4
aesthetic experience, 44
After Virtue, 7–8
Albert the Great, Saint, 71
American Constitution, 78, 79
American Founders, 81
Amin, Idi, 77
Anarchy, State, and Utopia, 81
ancien régime, 89, 94
Anscombe, Elizabeth, 81
anthropology, human, 20, 34, 39, 83, 100, 112
Aquinas, Saint Thomas, 2, 4, 36, 40, 41, 53–54, 56, 61, 64, 70–71, 74, 76, 78, 95, 97, 108, 109, 113
Aristippus, 35
Aristotle, 5, 35, 41, 43, 53, 56, 64, 71, 95, 97, 108, 113
Aron, Raymond, 115
associations, intermediate, 93–95, 96, 117
atheism, xiii–xiv

Augustine of Hippo, Saint, 39, 108
Austin, John, 3
authority, 72, 73–76, 77, 98, 111
autonomy, human, 51, 53, 56, 57–62

Balthasar, Hans Urs von, 115, 116
Bentham, Jeremy, 3, 15–17, 20, 22, 23, 25, 53
Bentham, Sir Samuel, 3
Berlin, Sir Isaiah, 9, 30–31, 46, 90
Boleyn, Ann, 117
British and Foreign Truth Society, 14
Brothers Karamazow, 111
Bourbon monarchy, 76–77, 94, 96
Boyle, Joseph, 99
Burke, Edmund, ix, xi, 8, 52, 93
Buttiglione, Rocco, 98, 99

Caiaphas, 84, 87
Caligula, 84
Castro, Fidel, 77
Catholic Church, 2, 7, 106, 109, 110, 114
Catholic Faith, 109, 112, 113, 114, 118
"Catholic Whig," 106–7, 108–9
Catholics, 105, 106, 108, 112

Centesimus Annus, 9
Christianity, 2, 4, 14, 71, 112
Church of England, 13
Cicero, 6, 95
civil society, 86, 93–96
cloning, 51
codified law, 64
coercion, 32–33, 58, 62–63, 81
Cold War, xiii
commerce, 94, 96–101
common good, 5, 59, 61,71–73, 77–78,
      83–84, 85, 100
common law, 64
communism, 33, 70
community, 59, 61, 100
Condillac, Abbé Etienne de, 3
consciousness, 38
consequentialism, 18
Constant, Benjamin, 7, 20, 80–81, 82
constitutionalism, 76–80, 90, 108, 117
Constitution of Liberty, 22, 32, 52
constructivism, 78–80
contract, 96, 97, 98, 101
Copleston S.J., Frederick, 18
Corn Laws, 14
culture, 54

Danton, Georges-Jacques, 110
Darwinism, 14
De Gaulle, Charles, 80, 81
death, 102
Declaration of Independence, 78
Declaration of the Rights of Man and
      the Citizen, 80
democracy, 74, 77, 86, 89–93, 101
Democracy in America, xi–xii, 101
deposit of faith, 109
Descartes, René, 38, 39
determinatio, act of, 78, 79, 83
determinism, 38
difference principle, 24
Dignitatis Humanae, 112
Dostoevsky, Fyodor, 111
Döllinger, Ignaz von, 2

Dubay, Thomas, 117
Dworkin, Ronald, 56–58

economics, 99–100
emotions, 29, 40–41
emotivism, 8
Engels, Friedrich, 95–96
England, 14
Enlightenment, French, 15, 94, 112
Enlightenment, Scottish, 95
equality, 91, 93, 94
experience, 74
Ethics, 35
euthanasia, 51, 113, 114
evolution, 79

family, 71, 74, 95
Faust, 34
feudalism, 96
Ferguson, Adam, 95, 96, 97
Finnis, John, xii, 4, 16–17, 19, 36, 40,
      56, 57, 65, 83
Fortescue, Sir John, 79–80
Foucault, Michel, 7
Fragment on Government, 15
Frankl, Victor, 45
free choice, xii, 9, 35, 37, 39–41,
      43–45, 47, 59, 74, 80, 85, 92, 97,
      102, 116, 117, 118
free market, 97–101
free will, 5, 37, 39–41, 49, 83, 111
freedom. *See* liberty.
French Revolution, xi, 8, 15, 20, 69,
      94, 110
French Republic, Fifth, 80
French Republic, Second, xi
friendship, 44, 63
Fuller, Lon, 65

Galston, William, 7, 56, 60–61, 113–14
Gaudium et Spes, 116
General Will, 77, 94
Gentz, Friedrich, 8
George III, 29

George, Robert P., xii, 14, 57, 81
Gladstone, William, 2
Glorious Revolution, 29, 80
God, xiii–xiv, 3, 81, 91, 102, 106, 107,
    111, 113, 114, 115, 116, 118
goods, basic, 42–45, 49, 62, 84, 90–91,
    98, 100, 101, 102, 116
goods, instrumental, 76
goods primary, 23, 24
government, 4, 72, 73–75
Gray, John, 25
Gregory of Nyssa, Saint, 42
Grisez, Germain, xii, 62, 74–75
Guizot, François, 52, 69, 90, 97

habeas corpus, 78
Habsburg monarchy, 77
Hampden, Renn Dickson, 13
harm principle, 20, 55
Hart, H.L.A., 52
Hayek, Friedrich von, 1, 6, 7, 8, 21–22,
    31–34, 41, 42, 52–53, 63, 64, 70,
    74, 79–80, 84, 87, 90, 111–12
health, 85
hedonistic calculus, 6, 16, 19
Hegel, G.W.F., 29, 32, 95, 96
Henry VIII, 117
Hitler, Adolf, xiii, 87
Hobbes, Thomas, 15, 35, 40, 53
Home Rule, 3
Homer, 29
homo economicus, 99–100
homosexuality, 113, 114
Human Action, 21, 41
human nature, 15, 19
Hume, David, 5, 15, 25, 34, 35, 40, 53,
    82

incommensurability, 16
integral fulfillment. *See* integral liberty
integral liberty, xiii, 9, 44, 46, 59, 61,
    72, 73, 74, 75, 82, 83, 86, 90, 92,
    94, 96, 101–2, 115, 117
Industrial Revolution, 14

Jardin, André, 6
Jesus Christ, 107, 109, 116
Journal intime, 20
John Paul II, 9
Judaism, 2, 4
justice, 7, 23, 63, 65, 74, 106

Kant, Immanuel, 80, 110–11
Keane, John, 96
Kelsen, Hans, 60
Kingdom of God, 106, 107, 108, 115,
    116, 117
knowledge, 44, 63
Kukathas, Chandran, 19

law, 47, 51–65, 71–72
Law, Legislation and Liberty, 22
legal positivism, 64
Lenin, I.V., 108
Letter to the Romans, 5
L'Ancien Régime et la Révolution, xi
liberalism, 1–2, 14, 56, 112–13, 117
liberty, xii–xiii, 3–9, 22, 23, 24, 26,
    29–34, 55–63, 80, 90–91, 92, 94,
    96, 100, 102, 111, 117
life, 44, 54, 78, 82, 83, 84, 85, 113
Lincoln, Abraham, 84
Livy, 29
Locke, John, 77, 82, 95
Loss and Gain, 14
Louis XVI, 84, 89
Louis-Napoleon Bonaparte, xi
Louis-Philippe I, xi
Lustiger, Jean-Marie, 38, 39

MacIntyre, Alasdair, 7–8
Mackie, John, 8
Madison, James, 93
Maggiolini, Alessandro, 107
Magisterium, 113
Maistre, Joseph de, 36, 79
Malesherbes, Lamoignon de, 89
Manent, Pierre, 93, 116
Marcus Aurelius, 20

marriage, 44, 60, 61, 65, 100, 114
Marx, Karl, xi, 29, 37, 38, 95, 96, 98
Marxism, 14, 100
material goods, 101
materialism, 117
majoritarianism, 91
Mephistopheles, 34
metaphysics, 15, 32, 116
Methodism, 13
Middle Ages, 14, 76, 96, 116
militarism, 25
Mill, John Stuart, xii, 2–3, 9, 13–15, 17–20, 22, 23, 25, 38, 41, 55
Mises, Ludwig von, 21, 41, 74
modern world, 96, 107–9, 117, 118
modernity, 106, 108, 109, 111, 112, 118
Montesquieu, Charles de, 51–65, 77, 96, 101
moral ecology, 4, 47, 53–55, 60, 74, 98–99, 100
More, Sir Thomas, 33, 70, 117
mores, 34, 114

Napoleon Bonaparte, xi, 20–21
narcotics, 51
nationalism, 25
natural law, xii, 21
Nazism, 25, 70
Newman, John Henry, 13–14, 117
Newton, Sir Isaac, 71
Nietzsche, Friedrich, 35
Novak, Michael, 106
Nozick, Robert, 81

On Liberty, 3
Original Position, 23

pain, 6, 15–17, 19
Paine, Thomas, 8
Papal Infallibility, 2, 13
Paul, Saint, 5, 108
parlements, 76–77, 96
passions, 5, 35, 52

Péguy, Charles, ix
person, human, 9, 38–39
philosophes, xiii, 3, 5, 94
Physiocrats, 95, 97
political community, 72, 73, 74–75, 86, 95
Political Liberalism, 55
Plato, xiv
play, 44, 100
pleasure, 6, 15–17, 19, 34, 99
pluralism, 7, 53, 55, 62–63, 73, 102
Pol Pot, 77
pornography, 51, 54
positive law, 65, 78
practical reasonableness, xii, 40, 44, 49, 63–65, 71, 91, 102, 107, 111, 114, 115
preference, 6, 99–100
prices, 72
Principles of Political Economy, 3
privacy, 82
profit, 97
progress, 33–34, 84, 110–11
prudence, 62, 73–75, 79, 80, 85
public order, 84
Pusey, E.B., 13

Rationale of Evidence, 3
rationalism, 5, 21, 35, 112
rationalization, 53
Ratzinger, Joseph, 35, 37, 42
Rawls, John, 1, 6, 7, 21, 22–25, 41, 52, 55–56, 58, 70, 81, 105
Raz, Joseph, 7, 42–43
Reason, xii, 1, 5, 15, 16, 25, 29, 33, 34, 38, 39, 40–41, 42–44, 77, 82, 89, 100
Reform Act 1832, 14
Reform Act 1867, 3
relationships, 71, 100
relativism, moral, 31, 117
religion, xiii, 43–44, 102, 105–18
religious liberty, right of, 81
Revelation, 112, 113, 114

rights, 37, 80–86
rights-talk, 82
Rights of Man, 8
Road to Serfdom, 8
Robespierre, Maximilian, 81, 84, 89
Röpke, Wilhelm, xiii, 98, 99
romanticism, 25
Rorty, Richard, 31
Rousseau, Jean-Jacques, 30, 77, 94
rule of law, 63–65, 108
rule of men, 64

Sade, Marquis de, 84
science, natural, 30, 37
Scripture, 107, 113
Scruton, Roger, 51
Searle, John, 7
secularism, 110–14
sensus fidei, 109
separation of powers, 79
Shaftsbury, Earl of, 106
skepticism, xiv, 25, 30, 34–38, 70
skillful performance, 44, 99
slavery, 83
socialism, 9, 74, 98
soft despotism, 86, 93–95, 101
Solon, 79
Solzhenitsyn, Aleksandr, 45
state, 4, 6, 59, 64, 69–87, 93, 94, 95,
    98–99, 117
Stalin, Joseph, xiii, 58, 77, 81
Stauffenberg, Claus von, 87
Strauss, Leo, 25
Stuart dynasty, 80
subsidiarity, 61

Taking Rights Seriously, 56
Terror, Jacobin, 89
Theory of Justice, 22, 81

Thomson, Judith Jarvis, 105
Tocqueville, Alexis de, xi–xii, 6–7, 13,
    35, 36, 54, 69, 79–80, 86, 89–90,
    91–93, 94, 95, 96, 98–99, 101,
    105, 110, 111, 114, 118
totalitarianism, 31, 64, 73
Tradition, 113
transcendent, 101–2, 115
truth, xiv, 30, 35, 36, 56, 109, 115–16,
    117
Turgot, Jacques, 97
tyranny, 65

unanimity, 72
United Nations Declaration of Human
    Rights, 81
United States Supreme Court, 33
utilitarianism, xiii, 3, 9, 14–26, 33, 85,
    99–100, 102, 117
Utilitarianism, 3
utility, 5, 6, 15, 19, 22, 23, 99, 115
utopia, 107

Vatican Council, First, 2, 114
Vatican Council, Second, 108, 112, 116
Veil of Ignorance, 23, 81
vice, 55
virtue, 42
Voltaire, 7

wealth, 23, 100
Weinreb, Lloyd, 82
Weimar Germany, xii
welfare state, 73–74, 98–99
Whig institutions, 108–9
work, 44, 99

ABOUT THE AUTHOR

SAMUEL GREGG is a moral philosopher who has written and spoken extensively on questions of ethics in public policy, jurisprudence, and bioethics. He has an MA in political philosophy from the University of Melbourne, and a Doctor of Philosophy degree in moral philosophy from the University of Oxford. He is the author of several books and monographs, including *Economics and Ethics: The Quarrel and the Dialogue* (1999), *Morality, Law, and Public Policy* (2000), and *Economic Thinking for the Theologically Minded* (2001). He is American editor for the Italian journal, *La Societa*, and American correspondent for the German daily broadsheet newspaper, *Die Tagespost*. He is Director of Research at the Acton Institute, a Visiting Professor at the John Paul II Pontifical Institute for Marriage and the Family within the Pontifical Lateran University, and a consultant for Oxford Analytica Ltd. In 2001, he was elected a Fellow of the Royal Historical Society.